D0506769

What others are saying...

"A must-read for B2B marketing professionals, New Product Blueprinting is loaded with new concepts and practices you'll not find elsewhere. Never before has a book better instructed marketers on how to connect the dots between market needs and new products. Dan Adams ably clears the fog from a world where B2B marketers often don't know if their new products will truly excite customers until they launch them. That's just too late."

- Solomon Lemma, Business Development Manager, Air Products & Chemicals

"New Product Blueprinting provided us with an innovative, systematic method of identifying our customers' needs. Blueprinting will shake up your preconceptions, and all too often your misconceptions, about what your customers want and replace them with hard, market-driven data. Imagine that!"

- Mark Charpie, Innovations Manager, DeVilbiss

"If you want your employees out interviewing customers and planning great new products when you're not looking—and who wouldn't?—pick up a copy of New Product Blueprinting. It provides the process and training you'll need in order to make it happen. This book will help you plan your attack with pinpoint accuracy and grow profitably in your target market segments."

- Bob Poletti, Vice President, Marketing, Michelman

"Read this book if you are interested in market-driven innovation and maximizing the productivity of your value creation processes. Once enlightened, you'll be quite dissatisfied with the way you've been doing things. In short, New Product Blueprinting is your ticket to a lot of hard work. But there is an upside: If you take its lessons to heart, not only will you have happier customers, you'll have a lot more of them. Thank you, Dan, for a great process that is helping our commercial team be much more externally focused. It's helped the culture of our team shift from being day-to-day 'account managers' to 'curious total customer value opportunity seekers'."

- Victor Maurtua, Global Pharmaceutical Excipients Director, FMC Corporation

"Dan Adams is, without a doubt, one of the most thorough strategic thinkers in the business world. This book will take you on a business trip that will end up being one of your most successful trips to date. Dan has put together a strategic agenda that challenges you to be prepared while also encouraging you to follow the plan that will eventually lead to successful and repeatable sales. I am lucky to consider Dan a business and personal friend who has helped me throughout my career. If you read this book... trust the strategic plan, and you too will be successful."

- Willis Reese, Global Director, Hexion Specialty Chemicals

"My favorite aspect of New Product Blueprinting is the discovery interview. Potential customers hate being sold what you already have. They much prefer being asked what they want, and that is a primary focus of Dan Adams' Blueprinting. Dan teaches you that by listening to what your customers want, you find out how to focus your product development against a real target. That way there are no unmet needs. The bottom line: Killing a new product development project before wasting valuable resources to develop a product that nobody wants is just as important as hitting a new product home run. And New Product Blueprinting will help you do that every time!"

- Charley Storms, President and CEO, Red Spot Paint & Varnish Co., Inc.

"There is no denying the passion Dan Adams has for New Product Blueprinting. But even more impressive than that is his dedication to helping companies succeed. His new book should be required reading for every B2B supplier. This is the way to ensure that you are creating products that your customers won't be able to resist."

- Jill Greathouse, Business Development Manager, SprayCore

"As the era of vertically integrated producers declined, there instead arose a chain of independent specialist producers. In this new situation, you need to be at the correct end of the chain to remain in touch with the changing needs of the end-customer. If, like most of us, you live somewhere else in the chain, this book is a must-read for you. Dan has done a masterful job of providing specific, proven techniques to help us understand customer needs—the first key step in making innovation profitable."

- Dr. Sudhir Hublikar, Vice President, Science & Technology, AGY

New Product Blueprinting

New Product Blueprinting

The Handbook for B2B Organic Growth

Dan Adams

AIM Press
Cuyahoga Falls, Ohio

First Edition

Publisher's Cataloging-in-Publication Data
Adams, Dan, 1955- ⌐
    New product blueprinting : the handbook for B2B organic growth / Dan Adams.
-- 1st ed.
        p. cm.
        Includes bibliographical references and index.
        LCCN 2007943589
        ISBN-13: 978-0-9801123-4-4 (hardcover)
        ISBN-10: 0-9801123-4-6 (hardcover)

        1. New products. 2. Industrial marketing. I. Title.

    HF5415.153.A33 2008   658.5'75
                            QBI07-600343

To my wife, Carol, who

encouraged me when I tired,

guided me when I drifted,

believed in me when I doubted.

Contents

Introduction   1

Part I: Overview

Chapter 1.   This Book Is for B2B... Not Consumer Goods   11
Chapter 2.   This Book Is for Builders... Not Decorators   21
Chapter 3.   This Book Is for Maximizing Profits   29
Chapter 4.   What Is New Product Blueprinting?   37

Part II: Five Principles

Chapter 5.   Principle 1: Avoid Incrementalism and Its Death Spiral   53
Chapter 6.   Principle 2: Upgrade Your New-Product Machine   61
Chapter 7.   Principle 3: Pick Your Battleground Markets Wisely   73
Chapter 8.   Principle 4: Use Customer Interviews for a Competitive Edge   81
Chapter 9.   Principle 5: Develop Your People... Transform Your Business   97

Part III: Seven Steps

Chapter 10.   Step 1: Market Research   115
Chapter 11.   Step 2: Discovery Interviews   131
Chapter 12.   Step 3: Preference Interviews   151
Chapter 13.   Step 4: Side-by-Side Testing   159
Chapter 14.   Step 5: Product Objectives   167
Chapter 15.   Step 6: Technical Brainstorming   177
Chapter 16.   Step 7: Business Case   185

Appendix: How AIM Can Help   197
Bibliography   199
Index   201

Acknowledgments

I am grateful to the many who have taught me, inspired me and helped me with this book. I have learned personally from several of today's thought leaders: Jim Hlavacek showed me how to help a business escape the gravity of internal thinking to become *driven* by the needs of its markets. I am indebted to Tony Ulwick for his brilliant insights on understanding the outcomes customers desire. I leaned heavily on Charlie Prather's mastery of the subject of idea generation. And I applied *some* of Dr. M. J. Kirton's boundless insights to improving problem-solving by teams.

Other thought leaders were more fortunate. Instead of bending their ears, I dog-eared the pages of their books and papers. Some of the most important include Clayton Christensen on sustaining and disruptive innovation, Edward McQuarrie on customer visits, Neil Rackham on selling by engaging customers, and Bob Cooper for his impressive research on the drivers of new product development success.

As you will read, this book is not an academic work. If it cannot be used to markedly change a business, it is simply a failure. In nearly three decades working inside large corporations, I learned the business of business-building from these leaders: Kees Verhaar demonstrated how a man with a clear, unwavering vision creates a business of significance. Sarah Coffin taught me how a leader employs a listening ear and deep respect for the individual. Steve Demetriou showed how far a leader can take an organization by holding himself and others accountable to high expectations.

Many friends—clients, colleagues and others—invested a great deal of themselves in making this book readable and usable. I sincerely thank Duncan Cathcart, Laura Colcord, Michelle Devereux, Sara Edison, Ann

Eiden, Deborah Hensley, Sudhir Hublikar, Gregg Motter, Tom Pavilon and Willis Reese for their invaluable insights. Special thanks go to Sudhir Hublikar. While many friends have added fuel to this fire, it was Sudhir who came into my office with the flint and steel so many years ago.

There's not enough room to thank them by name, but I have learned a great deal from those attending the workshops I conduct. The questions and comments flow freely at these affairs... and it's not always clear who the teacher is! The cumulative experience of these workshop attendees numbers in the tens of thousands of years: If you detect real-world wisdom in this book, you now know who deserves much of the credit.

Finally, I thank my family for their patience and support. During this all-too-consuming work, children have graduated and grandchildren have been born... but no complaints lodged. My wife, Carol, deserves my greatest measure of loving thanks. She selflessly encouraged me to make this book all it could be, even though she sacrificed the most in doing so. Her loving support will be cherished long after this book is out of print.

Dan Adams
dan.adams@aimtolead.com

Introduction

A New Approach
What's Ahead
What Really Matters

If your company could pick just one competency to truly master, what would it be? Acquisitions? Perhaps, but if you buy businesses and cannot grow them, you will just build a house of cards. How about operational efficiency, quality or service? These are important, but if others match you—and they usually do—you're in a race to the bottom of a commoditization spiral. I find most business leaders want profitable, sustainable top-line growth and look to new products to deliver this. Not product "tweaks," but differentiated products customers will pay top dollar for and competitors can't match anytime soon.

Now here is the interesting part: Differentiated products must be... different. Yet, many producers behave exactly as their competitors while hoping for different results. I don't hear business leaders say, "Our R&D staff is 20% smarter than competitors', so our new products usually win." And few plan to win by understanding customer needs better than their competitors... which would let them *aim* that R&D brainpower better. Instead, they rely on routine customer interactions by their sales force and a "fuzzy front end" in their product development process to somehow separate them from that surly pack of competitors.

A New Approach

Some companies are taking a different approach... developing radically new skills to understand their customers' needs in depths never before achieved.

This is not being done by a handful of voice-of-the-customer (VOC) experts, but by scores or even hundreds of commercial and technical people within these companies. The companies then become market-driven new product *machines*, launching products eagerly embraced by their customers. This is New Product Blueprinting—a seamless, reproducible process to develop products customers love, competitors respect and stockholders applaud.

New Product Blueprinting focuses on the early stages of new product development—an area that is at once critical and exasperating to business leaders. Differentiated new products are key to profitable organic growth... and the front end (determining *what* to develop) is key to these products.[1] Yet in an age when most manufacturing processes have been brought under control, this fuzzy front end remains an untamed frontier. Think of your new products as the battles that determine your company's fate: Most of these battles are won or lost in the front end. Learn how to win the vast majority of these and you will change who your company *becomes*.

Are you ready to go beyond one-size-fits-all methods or hand-me-down techniques from consumer goods practitioners?

New Product Blueprinting is designed for one type of business: It delivers the most advanced new product development methods available today... *but only for businesses selling to other businesses (B2B)*. B2B suppliers have remarkable advantages over consumer goods suppliers that have been largely ignored. Are you ready to go beyond one-size-fits-all methods or hand-me-down techniques from consumer goods practitioners? New Product Blueprinting will help.

New Product Blueprinting is more than a step-by-step process. New skills, tools and mind-set must also be acquired. All of these will be described for you in this book. Sustainable organic growth through new products and services is a devilishly complex subject. Simply put, we're seeing exciting success in the world's largest B2B corporations, and this is your invitation to consider how your company might benefit.

This book is not for everyone. It is for those delivering business-to-business products and services (B2B), not consumer goods (B2C). It is for those offering specialties, not commodities. It is for practitioners working to move their own companies forward, not new product theorists and academicians. And it is for those wishing to transform their business, not apply a short-term patch. Perhaps you are an R&D scientist hoping to work on projects customers really care about. Maybe you're a marketing professional eager to add science to your art. Or a business leader determined to win the innovation war, not just the productivity war. This book was written for you.

What's Ahead

Plan to absorb New Product Blueprinting in three parts: Part I explains why it is targeted only at B2B suppliers, and why it appeals to those with a "builder" mind-set striving to maximize long-term profits. Part I closes with an overview of the New Product Blueprinting process.

Part II introduces five principles. New Product Blueprinting—while not difficult—requires change. Frankly, no busy professional will change *anything* without compelling reasons. It is not good enough to harbor vague discontent with your new products and company growth. You need convictions about what *must* change. For many, a mental journey like this needs to be completed:

1. What's wrong? Many companies develop uninspired, undifferentiated products, and this commoditization is hurting them… or killing them if they have low-cost, off-shore competitors.

2. What should be fixed? The studies are done, the votes are counted and clearly most companies do poor up-front work (what you should do before entering the development stage).[2]

3. Where should we work? B2B suppliers often dabble in many markets. It is far better to segment these and launch an overwhelming assault on the most attractive market segments.

4. How should we work? Exciting new products call for exciting new methods—such as the Discovery Interview—to truly understand the customer's world and ensure an "outside-in" focus.

5. How do we make this happen? Nothing changes until people change. Real-world experience is showing certain approaches to be highly effective in driving implementation throughout an organization.

Part III will immerse you in the day-to-day practice of New Product Blueprinting. This is not an abstract idea: While you are reading this, teams are *doing* this, and Part III explains what they are doing. You'll move through all seven Blueprinting steps in detail to understand how and why the approach works. (While all seven steps are needed for major new products, individual steps can be applied as appropriate for smaller projects.)

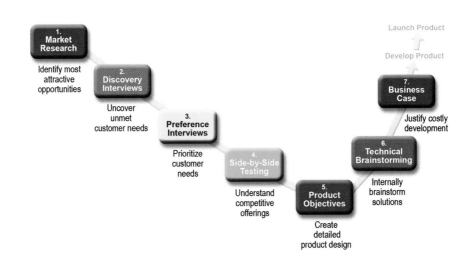

1. Market Research. New tools help you screen and target attractive market segments... so you can develop new products in the most fruitful areas.

2. Discovery Interviews. Technical-commercial teams interact with customers in a respectful, peer-to-peer fashion. Definitely not your father's VOC.

3. Preference Interviews. Out with internal bias and unsupported assumptions. In with hard data on what customers want most and how they measure it.

4. Side-by-Side Testing. A brutally frank look at competitors' products vs. yours. This baseline lets you attack their weak spots, avoid being blind-sided, and optimize your pricing.

5. Product Objectives. No more guessing at new product designs. You know exactly what customers want and competitors lack... so you can now design with confidence.

6. Technical Brainstorming. Next, match what you *want* to do with what you *can* do. You conduct this idea-generation internally, but draw on a heavy dose of innovation from outside your company.

7. Business Case. Think like a venture capitalist and explore 12 areas to drive out assumptions, bias, omission and wishful thinking before you begin heavy product development spending.

What Really Matters

I hope you enjoy this book. But if enjoyment was your chief goal, I doubt you'd pick this over a John Grisham novel. I hope you gain new knowledge. But just getting smarter doesn't seem all that smart, does it? Mostly, I hope this book helps you *shake up your company*.

For 29 years, I worked as an employee in the trenches of large B2B corporations. We were there for one reason: to deliver value to our customers. And customers got this value through our products. It boiled down to how much value our products delivered vs. the competition. We all realized this was the critical point on which our success turned... so over the long-haul we tirelessly focused on creating exciting new products for these customers.

Sure we did. Actually… we got lost more often than not. We got dragged into the day-to-day meat-grinder. We spent more time thinking about the effect (financials) than the cause (customer value). And we imagined that we could predict what customers wanted by sitting in conference rooms talking to ourselves. There is only one reason any company puts up with this: New product success is measured with a multi-year yardstick, and we were measuring ourselves with monthly and quarterly rulers. Since new products from years gone by can carry a business for years to come, this folly isn't obvious.

Occasionally, we got it right. If you have ever developed a new product customers rave about, you know how good this feels. What did not feel good was our inability to replicate the occasional success. If our manufacturing department made only every third product within specification, they'd be replaced. Yet we had accepted this hit rate as perfectly normal in our #1 job—creating customer value through our products.

And this brings us to what really matters. New Product Blueprinting is all about changing the DNA of your company so it *routinely* delivers more new product value than your competitors. Coming up with a new process—or a book that describes it—is the easy part. The tough part is implementation… getting people to do things differently day in and day out.

Will the short-term time and financial pressures go away while you make this change? Hardly. That's why you must concentrate the *best tools* on that part of your new product process *most in need of repair.* For over three decades, independent research has established that the most needy part is the front end.[3] So you know where to work.

What about finding the best tools? For B2B suppliers, the tools have been makeshift, borrowed, scattered about or completely missing. For years my passion has been to refurbish older tools and build brand new tools for this job. The result is New Product Blueprinting. These tools have now been proven worthy by trained craftsmen in hundreds of projects, and they're all stored in one toolbox for you.

This book explains these tools and shows you how they are used. We've made the last half detailed and transparent so you can pick up many ideas to improve your existing process. We've even included 20 screen shots of Microsoft Excel® [4] spreadsheets to "pull back the curtain" for you.

> Future competitive advantage will come from *what we design*, not how faithfully or efficiently we reproduce it.

These are tough times to shake up a company in the manner we've described. But exciting times. In the last decades of the 20th century, companies discovered they could reach unimagined levels of manufacturing quality and productivity. I believe the next frontier is to dramatically improve the way we develop new products. Future competitive advantage will come from *what we design*, not how faithfully or efficiently we reproduce it. Why be satisfied with great quality and productivity for making products customers yawn at... especially if competitors have the same quality and productivity.

As Statistical Process Control and Six Sigma were to operational improvement, New Product Blueprinting is to new product success. It requires an investment in people and a commitment to do things differently. But then, that's how we differentiate, isn't it?

Endnotes

1. The non-profit benchmarking organization, American Productivity and Quality Center, conducted a major new product development study in 2003 and concluded, "Customer research and market inputs is the strongest discriminator overall of the study's best-practice organizations." See Paige Leavitt, ed., *Improving New Product Development Performance and Practices* (Houston: APQC International Benchmarking Clearinghouse, 2003), 55.
2. More than 30 years of research suggests that inadequate market analysis is the leading cause of new product failures. (See end-note 1 in Chapter 4.) Yet, in the APQC study cited above, the researchers found, "A small minority of survey participants (11.4%) report that their product definitions are based on thorough market research with customers or users." See Paige Leavitt, ed., *Improving New Product Development Performance and Practices* (Houston: APQC International Benchmarking Clearinghouse, 2003), 24.
3. See end-note 1 in Chapter 4.
4. Excel is a registered trademark of The Microsoft Corporation.

Chapter

Part I: Overview

1. This Book Is for B2B… Not Consumer Goods
2. This Book Is for Builders… Not Decorators
3. This Book Is for Maximizing Profits
4. What Is New Product Blueprinting?

Part II: Five Principles

5. Principle 1: Avoid Incrementalism and Its Death Spiral
6. Principle 2: Upgrade Your New-Product Machine
7. Principle 3: Pick Your Battleground Markets Wisely
8. Principle 4: Use Customer Interviews for a Competitive Edge
9. Principle 5: Develop Your People… Transform Your Business

Part III: Seven Steps

10. Step 1: Market Research
11. Step 2: Discovery Interviews
12. Step 3: Preference Interviews
13. Step 4: Side-by-Side Testing
14. Step 5: Product Objectives
15. Step 6: Technical Brainstorming
16. Step 7: Business Case

Part I

Part I shows you where New Product Blueprinting fits, who it helps, and how it works... and provides insights into why it is so powerful.

Chapter 1

This Book Is for B2B...
Not Consumer Goods

Five Differences between Industrial Buyers and Consumers
Three New Goals for B2B Product Development
Four New Approaches for B2B Product Development

I once spoke with someone designing an industrial product that would be buried deep inside roofing shingles... where no consumer would even know it existed. She lamented, "I wish we were selling products directly to consumers so we could ask them what they wanted." She seemed surprised when I said, "But you have some advantages in the B2B world that consumer goods producers will *never* have."

Of course we all know there are differences between developing products for end consumers vs. other companies. Some of these differences show up during product launch: If you see any polyethylene terephthalate plastic advertised during the next Super Bowl, you can bet it will already be molded into a 2-liter soda bottle. And there are clear differences in how we design new products. If your B2B customers are in fierce competition with each other, don't try getting them together in a cozy focus group.

Yet I believe the chasm between B2B and B2C new product development (NPD) should be even wider than it is today. B2B suppliers have severely limited themselves—particularly in the front end of product development—by using B2C practices to understand customer needs. How have B2B suppliers limited themselves? How much better could they be at this? Should they modify B2C practices... or start over with a clean slate?

To answer these questions, we must understand the differences between B2B and B2C customers at their most fundamental levels. How different are they? After all, didn't the same guy who bought a rail car of soda ash on Friday buy a can of soda drink on Saturday?

Actually he changed... or at least his behavior did. As shown in Figure 1.1, there are five areas in which the soda drink buyer behaves differently from the soda ash buyer. To sort this out, let's go through a three-step process. We will begin with *observations* about B2B and B2C customer differences. Then we will discuss their *implications*, specifically how these differences should lead to new goals. Finally, we will present new *approaches*... B2B-tailored methods to deliver uncommon value to your customers and your bottom line.

If your B2B customer is not focusing her considerable skills on *your* product, it's probably because you haven't asked her to.

Before starting, we should recognize a *spectrum* of possible buying behaviors. Consumer goods are at one end and industrial goods at the other. We define the latter as a product used by another company to make its own product. A "mid-spectrum" example is selling new laptops to soda ash salesmen: still B2B, but somewhat closer to B2C. The principles in this book apply to all B2B situations, but are most pronounced when your product is an integral part of another company's process or product.

Five Differences between Industrial Buyers and Consumers

1. Technically Savvy. Expect more out of your customer interview with a hydraulic hose buyer than a garden hose buyer. You can have an intelligent, peer-to-peer conversation about hose durability, fluid specifications and pressure ratings because this is the hydraulic engineer's job. This engineer has the education, job experience and motivation: Your new product can make her a hero at work. If she's not focusing her considerable skills on *your* product, it's probably because you haven't asked her to.

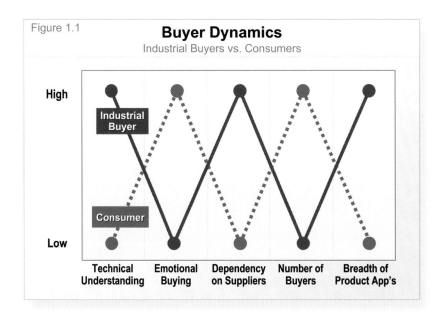

Figure 1.1

Buyer Dynamics
Industrial Buyers vs. Consumers

2. Emotional Buying. The consumer is emotional—some would say impulsive and fickle—in his buying decisions. As affluent consumers, few of our buying decisions are based on hard economics. And we are held *accountable* for even fewer buying decisions. (If we were, those rows of storage rental units would never have sprouted.) The industrial buyer, though, justifies his decisions on economics, consults with others, and knows his decisions may be questioned later. It's amazing how rational we can be if we really must.

3. Supplier Dependency. If the office supply store is out of your favorite brand of paper, you simply reach for another. If you are a paper manufacturer, though, you depend on your pigment supplier to provide you with uniform product and on-time deliveries. And that pigment supplier can make you a winner within your company if their new pigment lets you increase line speed or produce a brighter white.

4. Number of Buyers. If you are selling toothpaste, you could have millions of buyers. If you are selling print paste, you may have dozens. This difference is important in new product launches, and influences the promotional tools you choose. It also drives one of the most powerful and overlooked benefits in B2B product development: *buyer engagement*. For as much as the consumer-products company might wish to do so, it isn't practical to engage millions of toothpaste consumers in product design.

5. Breadth of Applications. The last difference doesn't always apply, but is common enough to consider. Generally, the closer a product is to the end of the value chain (final consumer), the more specialized and narrow its applications. Consumers use food coloring for… well… coloring food. But B2B customers use colorants in plastics, nail polish and pharmaceutical pills. Most B2B suppliers sell into many different applications, and these often vary greatly in profit potential, growth rate, and other key characteristics.

Three New Goals for B2B Product Development

Careful reflection of these five customer differences leads to three new goals during the front end of B2B new product development (Figure 1.2).

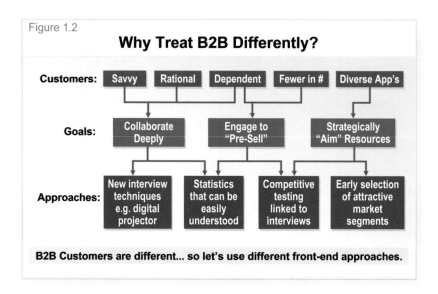

Figure 1.2

Why Treat B2B Differently?

B2B Customers are different… so let's use different front-end approaches.

1. Collaborate Deeply with Customers. Because B2B buyers are more technically savvy, the depth is possible. Because B2B buyers are more rational, the collaboration is worthwhile. And because B2B buyers are more supplier-dependent, their time is available. Unlike a consumer focus group, in which participants are paid for their views, B2B suppliers often have close relationships with customers who are willing to speak their minds.

If you properly engage customers, they will bring attributes into your product design you would have never considered. In a study of well-conducted B2B interviews by Hewlett-Packard, 76% of the practitioners reported their interviews led to unexpected or surprising information.[1] Now that's how product leaders gain a competitive edge: by getting past their preconceived notions and putting themselves in a position to be *surprised* by the customer. With New Product Blueprinting, technical and commercial people learn skills for uncovering not just spoken needs, but unspoken and even unimagined needs. Unimagined needs surface when the customer is asked intelligent, probing questions and is engaged in a collaborative, peer-to-peer dialogue with a highly skilled supplier.

2. Engage Customers to Pre-Sell. Nothing makes someone want to buy a new product as much as helping to design it. Over a 12-year period, the Huthwaite Corporation observed 35,000 sales calls and made some fascinating observations.[2] Here's what they found for the sale of large-ticket items: If the salesperson just described product *features*—facts, data, characteristics—the impact was neutral to slightly negative. If the salesperson explained *benefits* the product offered the customer, the impact was slightly positive. But if the salesperson asked the customer for explicit needs, and then described how their product met them, the success rate skyrocketed.

> Take the most powerful sales technique available, make it more genuine, and use it much earlier.

Now let's think about this: You are a salesperson calling on me and you ask what I want. After I respond, you reach into your briefcase, pull out a brochure and say, "What a coincidence. That is exactly what I'd like to sell you!" Even though I know you are just here to sell me (you're a salesperson after all) I'm now much more likely to buy from you. What if you applied this psychology *before* you designed your product, when customers knew their input really mattered? Imagine if your design engineer probed key customers' needs, stayed in touch during product design and came back later with a product prototype. Customers would be interested because you'd be bringing them *their* new product. You would be taking the most powerful sales technique available, making it more genuine, and using it much earlier. You'd be selling your product before you designed it!

Here is where the smaller number of B2B customers helps: You couldn't engage millions of toothpaste consumers, but imagine what you could do with your ten largest print paste customers. This "engagement potential" is a great advantage in B2B product development... and it is grossly under-used by most B2B producers. New Product Blueprinting not only engages customers, it impresses them with an interviewing process that is logical and focused on them. What customer doesn't want to work with a supplier who is competent and cares about them? So powerful is this effect that it often puts that supplier in a different light immediately, sometimes leading to ancillary sales well before the new product is developed.

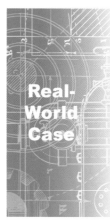 **Real-World Case** A business was holding its global sales meeting shortly after receiving its initial training in New Product Blueprinting. One overworked sales rep questioned, "Do we really have time for Blueprinting?" A marketing colleague from the United Kingdom replied, "I think we'd better *make* time. For several years I've been trying to get just one project going with a certain prospect. Last week we had a Discovery Interview with them. They were so impressed, I left the meeting with six projects!"

3. Strategically "Aim" Resources. Clever consumer-goods producers routinely segment their markets, but they have to work hard for modest gains. Ultimately, their market segments are still *people*, and socio-economic differences only go so far. For most B2B products we've worked with—from argon gas to zinc coatings—some market segments are very attractive and others are not. The range of attractiveness is often startling, with customers in multiple segments paying quite different prices for similar products.

Most B2B suppliers don't differentiate enough between market segment opportunities. They aim too many resources at slow-growth, dog-eat-dog segments and too few at the most attractive. The first step in New Product Blueprinting is targeting the best market segments. What's the point of aiming scarce resources at a stagnant segment dominated by an entrenched competitor, or about to be attacked by low-cost, off-shore producers?

Four New Approaches for B2B Product Development

Collaboration, pre-selling and strategically-aimed resources are fine goals, but you can't reach them without new approaches. You don't need consumer-oriented VOC techniques such as tape-recording and observing your customers through one-way mirrors. You want them feeling like professionals whose advice is being sought by a peer... not chimps being observed by Jane Goodall. Your customers are smart. If you work *with* them, they will make you smarter. New Product Blueprinting uses four approaches tailored specifically for doing this in the B2B world:

> Your customers are smart. If you work *with* them, they will make you smarter.

1. Digital Projection. Use a laptop and digital projector to display everything you record during customer interviews. This lets several participants work together in an idea-generation environment. You will be amazed at how engaged customers become when they don't have to guess what you're scribbling or typing to yourself.

Customers really *engage* when they see their ideas projected.

A new client explained why they had selected New Product Blueprinting: "We had been interviewed by others using typical voice-of-the-customer approaches. A couple of weeks later we received their transcripts. Some of it was wrong and frankly, we were on to other matters by then. But when someone interviewed us using New Product Blueprinting, we felt we were part of the process. We could see what was being recorded and make corrections on a real-time basis."

2. Simple Statistics. We need to get quantitative about the attributes our customers want in our next new product. But we don't need to get carried away with over-the-top statistics. How engaged will your customers be if they can't understand why one product attribute was selected over another? And without *their* understanding, it won't be *their* product design. With New Product Blueprinting, you will ask them for satisfaction and importance ratings that are simple, effective and easily understood.

3. Competitive Testing. Teams often charge down the product development path without testing competitors' capabilities. You can't ask that garden hose consumer for help on side-by-side test procedures, but you certainly can ask the hydraulics hose engineer. If you follow up with her tests, you will a) continue to engage her, b) avoid getting blind-sided by competitors, c) find competitive vulnerabilities to attack in your design, and d) set optimal pricing. Competitive testing helps you quantitatively understand all the options from the customer's perspective; skip this and you will probably leave money on the table when you set your new product price.

4. Market Segmentation. B2B producers will have the best return on their NPD resources if they pass three market segmentation tests very early: First, a well-defined cluster of customers with similar needs (a.k.a. market segment) has been targeted. Second, the segment is worth winning in terms of size, profit potential, growth, etc. Third, the segment is "winnable," that is, not well-defended by a powerful, entrenched competitor.

Consumer goods producers find diminishing competitive advantage in effective but well-worn techniques such as focus groups. But Blueprinting approaches are not yet standard practice among B2B producers, so you can use them to build strong competitive leads. As a near-term bonus, we've seen clients impress their customers and boost credibility as soon as they begin. So take heart if your new product will be buried in a shingle.

A Word about "Products" and "Customers"

Have you ever met with insurance agents or bankers who said they had a new product for you? On a recent airline flight, the videotaped CEO said he hoped I would like their product. (How cool, I thought: I get an airplane!) In these cases, the "product" is a service. This broad use of the term is appealing, because it lets us describe *any* offering that provides value to the customer. It may be a physical article, but many have used New Product Blueprinting to develop new services or business models. Because this process begins by focusing on unmet customer needs instead of supplier solutions, it is ideally suited to lead you to any type of "product" the customer will care about.

We'll also use "customer" in a broad sense. We may be referring to an existing customer, a prospective customer, a former customer or a customer's customer. While New Product Blueprinting addresses differences in each of these, for simplicity we often refer to "customer" as anyone in our potential downstream value chain who could influence and benefit from our new "product."

Endnotes

1. Edward F. McQuarrie, *Customer Visits: Building a Better Market Focus, 2nd Edition* (Thousand Oaks, CA: Sage Publications, 1998), 28-29. We are indebted to McQuarrie, who contributed greatly to the subject of customer interviews through his work beginning in the late 1980's. In this reference, he surveyed more than 200 Hewlett-Packard practitioners about their experiences conducting customer visits. 90% of the respondents stated that these customer visits had a "direct impact on the products and services offered to customers."

2. Neil Rackam, *SPIN Selling* (New York: McGraw-Hill, 1988), 99-110. Rackham's classic work on selling is particularly appropriate for B2B in that his re-

search focused on "major sales"—those that require rational justification, involve inputs from several people, and are associated with serious consequences for the decision-maker. His first two SPIN steps—Situation and Problems—align perfectly with the first two elements of the Discovery Interview—Current State and Problems. While this was a coincidence, it led us to the notion that good B2B new product interviews could engage customers and effectively begin the "selling" process before the product was even developed.

Chapter 2

This Book Is for Builders...
Not Decorators

Decorators, Realtors and Landlords
Applying the Tools of Resolve and Skill
New Product Development for the Builder
Learning the Building Trade
Which End of the Machine Do You Work On?

One of the best compliments I ever heard given to a business leader was, "He's a builder." If you run a business, you have many roles. But peel them all back and look to the core that defines you, the purpose that drives you, and you're either a builder—or you're not. If you see a business that has steadily grown over the years in size, profitability and stature... look for the builder. If you see a business whose products have left competitors' products in the dust... look for the builder. If you see a business that grinds through the hard work of delivering real customer value, brushing aside fads, downturns and criticisms... look for the builder.

If you are a builder, there's a good chance this book will become dog-eared. It was written for you. It is loaded with practical suggestions on how to organically grow a B2B business through new products and services. Moreover, it's assembled in a proven, step-by-step process, so everyone in your organization can follow the same road map. That's important. Some leaders read a book and tell their direct reports to "make it happen." Builders know there is a wide gulf between nodding their heads around a conference room table and reaching the point where employees are actually *doing* it.

If you want hundreds of employees out interviewing customers and planning great new products when you're not looking, you'd best think this through. You need a process. You need training. This book is designed to help you plan your attack with pinpoint accuracy. If you are a builder.

Decorators, Realtors and Landlords

Let's be frank: Not everyone is a builder. Some are interior decorators. They are mainly concerned with making the place look good. For them, the "open house" sign is up with every quarterly financial report and someone is always looking. But running a business based on financial results is like driving a car by watching the painted road lines in your rear-view mirror. Most of what you are looking at has already happened. Builders look down the road, lean forward in their seats and drive with their high-beams on. No one is saying financial appearances are unimportant, but here is the question: Are you putting a coat of paint on a finished house, or keeping a busy *building* site neat and orderly?

> If you don't know how to grow them, acquisitions are a house of cards at best, and the business equivalent of a Ponzi scheme at worst.

Still other business executives are realtors. Their hearts are in buying and selling; they reap reward when the work of others' hands *changes* hands. To be fair, sometimes their industry is ripe for consolidation, or the deal is part of a solid growth plan. But often the leader never learned the "building" trade on the way up, or is too impatient to construct something of lasting value. Even if the acquisition is successful—certainly not a given—the

You are a Builder if...		
You Are Probably A...	**If Your Main Passion Is...**	**And Your Main Timeframe Is...**
Builder	Organic Growth	Years
Interior Decorator	Financial Reporting	Months & Quarters
Realtor	The Deal	Months & Quarters
Absentee Landlord	Personal Interests	Days & Weeks

leader had better know how to grow it afterwards.[1] The alternative is to keep making more acquisitions—a house of cards at best and the business equivalent of a Ponzi scheme at worst.

The Builder's Tools... Resolve and Skill

There are other roles. One is the absentee landlord; he maintains his property but his interests reside in a different neighborhood. Perhaps you have met executives who apply themselves at work, but their hearts are at the country club. Does this mean you're not a builder if you've executed acquisitions, try to present a good company image, or enjoy golf? Absolutely not. You can do all these and be a builder. Builders distinguish themselves not by individual events, but by their relentless pursuit of a goal. When you observe builders, you see they have a clear picture of what they wish to create and employ two tools to accomplish their vision: resolve and skill.

Applying the Tools of Resolve and Skill

What separates the construction of a glorious cathedral from a rough shed? The cathedral builder knows he will need unswerving resolve to finish his masterpiece. He has counted the cost in years and is willing to pay it to create something of enduring value. Other projects may require attention, but the builder is not deterred from creating his cathedral. The shed maker moves from project to project, living for today, caring little about his legacy. When you see a business leader chasing the quick fix or current fad, you're not looking at a builder.

Once the cathedral builder has committed resolve to his project, he then commits skill. He recruits the finest stone masons and wood carvers he can find, and apprentices more for the future. Because these craftsmen know the passion of the builder, they work with pride, secure in the knowledge they have employment until the cathedral is finished. The shed maker can hire unskilled laborers from the local tavern whose goals match his: finish their work and collect their pay. When you see a leader unwilling to attract talent and invest in new skills, you're not looking at a builder.

New Product Development for the Builder

Builders are committed to developing exciting new products because they know it's the best way to avoid that slow-motion train wreck called commoditization. While other leaders are looking in the rear-view mirror or down the fairway, the builder can see this train coming and wants *nothing* to do with it.

A reverse auction is the business version of "Scared Straight." Have you ever watched an internet-based reverse auction? During the bidding session, several suppliers sit at their computers and keep lowering their prices for a pre-established piece of business. Finally at the end, panic reigns, the bottom drops out and the "winning" supplier takes all. Do you remember "Scared Straight"—a crime deterrence program that scheduled short prison visits for troubled youth? A reverse auction is the business version of this, and should be watched by any leader letting a specialty business grow stale. Since the process works only with undifferentiated products, you'll know you've already been "commoditized" if your customer invites you to one of these.

Builders are mindful of the never-ending tug-of-war between specialty and commodity products. On one hand, the passage of time naturally leads to commoditization as products move through their life cycle (Figure 2.1). Competitors introduce me-too products, and purchasing agents do all they can to commoditize products through standardized specifications and price negotiations. On the other hand, several forces lead to specialty products: uncovering unmet customer needs, meeting them with differentiated products and selling based on value-in-use, not unit price.

Figure 2.1

Specialty vs. Commodity
Forces in Constant Tension

Specialty	Semi-Specialty	Commodity

Forces Pulling to Specialty

- **Understanding customers' unmet needs**
- **Introducing high-value differentiated products**
- **Selling based on customer value-in-use**

Forces Pulling to Commodity

- **The passage of time (product life-cycles)**
- **Competitors introducing me-too products**
- **Purchasing agents negotiating unit prices**

Specialty forces all come from the supplier... or they don't come at all.

Consider two principles of commoditization: First, it is in the best interests of your customers and competitors to commoditize your existing products, so the forces pulling your company toward specialty will come from you... or they won't come at all. Second, the commoditization of existing products can be slowed but never stopped. The waves will eventually level your sand castles, so you must always be building new ones. And this is the wisdom of the builder: Always keep building new products. Build them well, build them high, build them away from the surf... but never stop building.

> Forces pulling your company toward specialty will come from you... or they won't come at all.

Learning the Building Trade

New Product Blueprinting can help you become a better builder. You will begin by surveying potential building sites. These are market segments— clusters of customers with similar needs—for whom you'll create exciting new products. Don't pick sites overbuilt with entrenched competitors. Re- member "location, location, location," as you target segments with favor- able trends and good fit with your capabilities. Dig the foundation deep by interviewing customers to understand their most important unmet needs.

Which End of the Machine Do You Work On?

For me, the ultimate test of a builder is to watch which end of the machine he's working on. Let me explain. One of my first jobs as a freshly-minted chemical engineer was as night shift foreman. The process began with petrochemicals and ended with a perpetual strip of rubber coming from the extruder die. My job was to test the rubber; if anything was wrong I immediately began checking what was going into the machine's feed hopper.

Twenty-five years later, as I sat through my umpteenth financial business review, it dawned on me: We're all standing around the extruder die where the product comes out. We don't like what the machine is producing, so we're exhorting it to do better and fussing with the outlet die a bit. But nobody's checking the feed hopper!

Of course, it *looked* like we were having an intelligent meeting. We talked about our gross margins, price increases and growth rates. But these had been determined years earlier, largely by our new products. If we had fed well-planned, high-value new product projects into the hopper, the meeting would be completely different than if we had fed ill-conceived or undifferentiated projects. By the time of our meeting, we could talk about what came out… but we couldn't *change* it much.

The builder knows this and spends most of his time at the feed hopper. He feeds in technology that will be used to create exciting new products. He feeds in an organization that is motivated to build for the future. He feeds in capabilities and training needed to uncover customers' most important unmet needs. Sure, he still spends some time at the extruder die examining the output. But his heart is at the feed hopper because then he *knows* what will come out the other end.

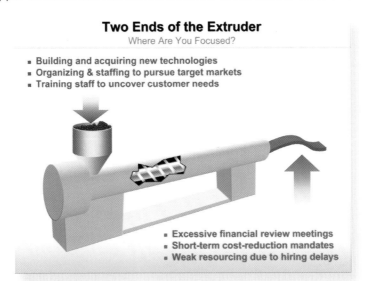

Two Ends of the Extruder
Where Are You Focused?

- Building and acquiring new technologies
- Organizing & staffing to pursue target markets
- Training staff to uncover customer needs

- Excessive financial review meetings
- Short-term cost-reduction mandates
- Weak resourcing due to hiring delays

With the right building sites, skilled workers and enough time, you'll become known as a great builder. A word of advice: Don't spend too much time looking for "builder" qualifications in others. Instead, look where you can make the most difference. Yourself. Start with an audit of where you invest your time… at the feed hopper or the outlet die. Then plan your building projects, count the cost, and pick up your tools.

Endnotes

1. Considerable research has been completed on acquisition performance, and the news is not heartening: An A.T. Kearney study showed 58% of deals reduced shareholder value two years after the deal (115 large deals, 1993-1996). Boston Consulting Group found 60% reduced value one year later (302 large deals, 1995-2001). McKinsey reported that 70% of deals reduced or maintained shareholder value (193 deals, 1990-1997). Research also suggests that top management often does not fully understand or accept their own performance regarding acquisitions. In a KPMG study of 700 deals at 188 companies (1997-1999), 82% of the surveyed executives considered their acquisitions successful. In fact, only 30% added value, 39% showed no change and 31% lowered value. For more on these and other studies, see Alexandra Reed Lajoux, *The Art of M&A Integration, 2nd Edition* (New York: McGraw-Hill, 2006), 12-14.

Chapter 3

This Book Is for Maximizing Profits

Four Failure Modes
Changing Your Company
What Does Success Look Like?

Have you noticed that all new products are not created equal? On one hand, there is the occasional product that just won't stop. For years or even decades, it delivers enormous profits, carrying whole businesses and careers on its sturdy shoulders. And then there are the tired, the poor, the huddled masses of wretched new products you *wish* were on your competitors' teeming shores.

What separates them? Unless we sort this out, we can count on only more of the same. There is actually a science—a body of truths that can be observed and systematically arranged—to making money with new products. Our work indicates a highly profitable new product blockbuster must meet six conditions, not just four or five. That would be like getting four or five digits right in a six-digit lottery… after you've paid a lot of money to play.

Here are the conditions: A customer need *exists* that is *uncovered* by the supplier, the supplier *develops* and *delivers* a solution, and the supplier *captures* and *protects* this new value. See Figure 3.1 for a complete description. It is rare for a product to hit all of these, and there are many possible failure modes. But like products, failure modes are not created equal. Some are more common and damaging than others. Let's consider four of the most critical failure modes so we can be intentional about avoiding them.

Figure 3.1

Conditions for New Product Blockbusters

Condition	Description
Need Exists	Customers in target market segment have important needs not currently satisfied.
Need Uncovered	Suppler identifies and understands important, unsatisfied customer needs.
Solution Developed	Suppler develops a solution capable of addressing important, unsatisfied needs.
Solution Delivered	Supplier produces, distributes and supports solution so that customer needs are satisfied.
Value Captured	A price point is established that delivers a substantial portion of the value to the supplier.
Value Protected	The supplier effectively blocks all other suppliers from offering solutions at comparable pricing.

Four Failure Modes

Failure #1: Don't Bother... *Please.* In this case, customers in the target market segment are generally content; no significant unmet need exists today. (Sure, they could always use a lower price: That never goes away, does it?) It would be foolish to spend a lot of resources developing a major new product for this segment, since they're not going to pay for it. Does it still happen? *All* the time. As illustrated below, the supplier develops a solution

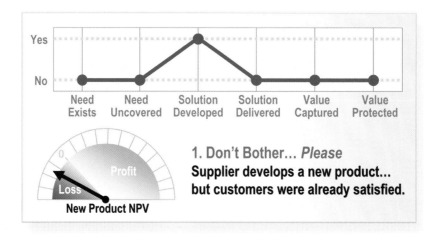

1. Don't Bother... *Please*
Supplier develops a new product...
but customers were already satisfied.

for a non-existent need—creating negative net present value (NPV) from project spending. (Note: The only time you should ever develop a major new product for this market is when you have protected technology that lets you dramatically lower pricing… a situation called low-end disruption by Clayton Christensen.[1])

Failure #2: Nice Shot, Wrong Target. Here the customers have very real unmet needs. Unfortunately, our out-of-touch supplier misses these, and instead develops a product based on internal, preconceived notions and a desire to push his really cool technology. The supplier comes up with a lovely solution to the wrong problem, a wonderful answer to a question never asked. This is a common occurrence in companies lacking the interest, effort or ability to explore their customers' worlds. Over and over our clients are surprised during interviews by what their customers want… and don't want. If the repairman fixed your washing machine when your dryer was broken, would you pay him? Neither will these customers.

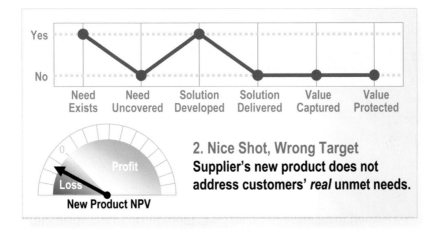

2. Nice Shot, Wrong Target
Supplier's new product does not address customers' *real* unmet needs.

Failure #3: Right Product, Wrong Price. Now our supplier is doing better: Customers are happy because he uncovered and met their important needs. Maybe too happy. He identified their needs, but did not understand the value he was about to deliver. As a result he left a lot of money on the table when he priced his product. This too is quite common: It takes some skill and work to uncover *what* customers really want… and then a little more to understand *how much* they'll benefit when you give it to them.

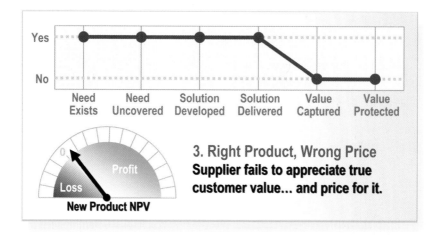

3. Right Product, Wrong Price
Supplier fails to appreciate true
customer value... and price for it.

Failure #4: Here Today, Gone Tomorrow. Serious NPV is now being generated by the supplier due to good market homework, good problem-solving and good pricing. This has not gone unobserved by competitors. Unfortunately, our supplier failed to block them with patents or other means... preventing a good financial story from becoming a great one. It takes a steady hand to protect new products for the long term in the face of short-term pressures. But the profits gained in coming years by doing so are often staggering. We see this with pharmaceutical companies, whose stock prices closely reflect their pipeline of protected new products under development. The same would be true for other companies except that their pipelines are far less transparent than that dictated by the federal drug approval process.

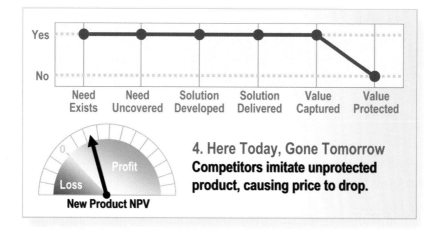

4. Here Today, Gone Tomorrow
Competitors imitate unprotected
product, causing price to drop.

Changing Your Company

You can apply this thinking to your businesses in two ways. The first is to employ a six-point checklist with your projects, so you don't *almost* get all six right. Not bad, but the second approach can have a far more substantial impact: Change the DNA of your company so project teams habitually drive for all six.

Well now, doesn't that sound simple? Actually, it isn't so complex when you notice a repeating pattern in each of the four failure modes: *It's all about the up-front work.* Put another way, the left side of each failure-mode graph drives the right side:

1) ***Don't Bother… Please:*** You should *quantitatively* test to see if a market segment is already content before spending a dime in product development. No excuses now: This can easily be done with a few B2B customer interviews.

2) ***Nice Shot, Wrong Target:*** Use these same interviews to probe for unspoken needs… and quantitatively measure how much customers want each need. Don't even think about solving a need unless you know customers truly care about it.

3) ***Right Product, Wrong Price:*** Some companies fixate on squeezing higher prices from tired old products. That's fine, but there is more juice in understanding customers' needs early. This lets you price new products to fully capture that value.

4) ***Here Today, Gone Tomorrow:*** When you carefully explore customers' worlds, you're more likely to find non-obvious needs.[2] Since competitors have not been working on these, this often leads to patentable solutions and protected pricing for you.

What Does Success Look Like?

There are actually two success modes, not one. The obvious one is Success Mode A, in which the supplier "rings the bell" on all six conditions. Deliver just a few more of these and you'll be wildly successful.

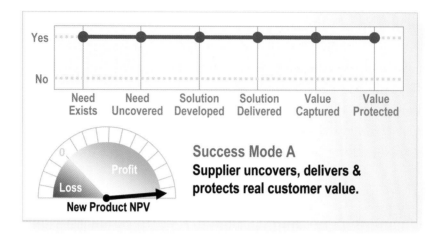

Success Mode A
Supplier uncovers, delivers &
protects real customer value.

But don't ignore Success Mode B: You thoroughly search the market segment but don't find any unmet needs—or any you could solve—so you move on to something else. You'll incur a small cost from secondary research and customer interviews, but it will be tiny compared to developing and launching a product no one wants. Make more of these "learning investments" than your competitors, and they won't be able to keep up with you.

Your unwillingness to walk degrades your ability to win.

Just walking away may not sound heroic, but until you do this, you won't have nearly enough resources to work on Success Mode A. Remember: Your unwillingness to walk degrades your ability to win. So encourage teams to drop projects customers don't care about. Celebrate Success Mode B and step briskly on to the next opportunity.[3]

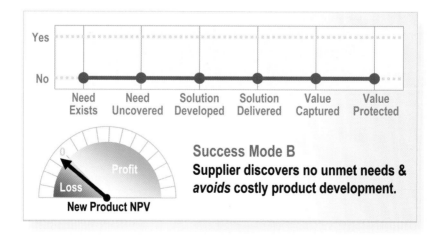

Success Mode B
Supplier discovers no unmet needs &
avoids costly product development.

Today, the story of new product development is a story of wasted resources and opportunities. As with quality and productivity improvements in recent decades, that story will certainly change in the future. But today at least, you can easily waste fewer resources and opportunities than your competitors. While that may not sound inspirational, it *is* a powerful competitive edge. Just tip the scale a bit from failure modes to success modes with solid up-front work.

Endnotes
1. Clayton M. Christensen and Michael E. Raynor, *The Innovator's Solution*, (Boston: Harvard Business School Press, 2003), 46. The authors describe two types of innovation: sustaining and disruptive. In the first case, suppliers make better products that can be sold at higher prices; incumbents usually win these battles. They cite two types of disruptive innovation: 1) Low-end disruptions, where a lower-cost product begins by nibbling at the bottom of the main-stream market, and 2) new-market disruptions, in which a product provides value to a population that had not been previously served in this way. Disruptive innovation is more likely to be offered by "upstart" players. All three types of innovation can be pursued using New Product Blueprinting, which helps you understand what your target market segment does and does not value. However, if a target segment is already satisfied (no significant unmet needs are uncovered), the only rational strategy is low-end disruption.
2. The power of working on customers' *non-obvious* needs has not been broadly and fully appreciated, in our opinion. For a more complete discussion, please see the inset at the end of Chapter 8, *"Theory of Non-Obviousness."*
3. Of the many advantages of New Product Blueprinting (high-impact products that address unmet customer needs, closer relationships with key accounts, etc.), one of the first B2B suppliers see is that they stop working on dead-end projects earlier... which frees up precious resources. Teams often bring favorite projects to training workshops that are already consuming considerable resources. In many cases, Blueprinting *quantitatively* reveals that customers are totally disinterested in these projects. While a bit disconcerting at first, this is a great way to free up resources to develop new products customer *will* care about.

Chapter 4

What Is New Product Blueprinting?

You Are the Architect
You Can Do More in B2B
Seven Blueprinting Steps
Is This Too Much Work?
Search Now... Sell and Solve Later
It's All About Customer Outcomes
New Product Blueprinting: What's Different?
New Skills and Tools Needed

Imagine you are having a house built. When finished you might say, "I wish we had run wiring for outdoor patio speakers," or "Too bad the evening sun washes out our TV screen." On the other hand, you might routinely hear guests say, "What a great idea! I never would have thought of *that.*"

What's the difference? *Creative foresight and a detailed plan.* With creative foresight, you develop a crystal-clear picture of your finished home in your mind before the first block is laid. Foresight does not develop quickly; you'll need time... and help. An architect might spend hours asking you questions such as:

- What hobbies does your family enjoy?
- How do you entertain guests?
- What type of cooking do you do?

Let's say you now have a picture of this dream home in your mind. Are you done? Hardly. You must communicate that picture to your builder, and that requires a detailed plan—a blueprint. Scribbled notes and arm-waving cannot transfer nearly enough information to ensure that your foresight *becomes* your home.

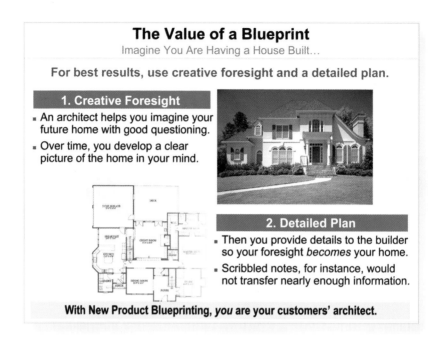

You Are the Architect

With New Product Blueprinting, your customers are the homeowners, and you are the architect. You patiently and expertly work with them to create a mental picture of something that will excite them. Then you reduce this creative foresight to a detailed plan the builder can execute. This is rather important because, as it turns out, you also happen to be the builder. Here is the interesting part: Unlike a homeowner who signs a contract with the builder, your customers can wait until your product is finished and reject it if they don't like it!

You would think this would make B2B producers very nervous... so nervous they would be absolutely certain of what customers wanted before "breaking ground." You would think. In fact, many hold meetings to decide internally what their customers want. Others develop new technology and push it at their customers. Still others keep building the same thing over and over, making minor tweaks from time to time.

When pressed about this strange state of affairs, some producers say they don't know *how* to uncover what their customers want. That's a fair assessment and one we hope to remedy in this book. Others say that customers don't know—and therefore can't tell them—what they want. I believe that's a wrong assessment and one we should address.

You Can Do More in B2B

It may seem that consumer goods buyers don't know what they want: They'll just recognize it when they see it. But buyers of B2B goods nearly always know what your product should accomplish. They may not be able to tell you *how* your product should do it, but that's really your job as the supplier, isn't it? When a B2B buyer considers how your product impacts his world, he can bring to bear his formal education, years of job experience, hours of focused attention and the personal motivation to succeed in his career… powerful forces largely missing in the consumer goods buyer.

In most cases, though, the B2B buyer does not bring these impressive resources to bear, *because the supplier doesn't ask him to*. Imagine if your architect stopped in to see you for half an hour, spent 15 minutes talking about the big game, and the rest of the time showing you pictures of houses he had built for others. Later, when the house failed to please you, he dismissed it saying, "Well, that buyer just didn't know what he wanted."

> Buyers of B2B goods nearly always know what your product should accomplish.

New Product Blueprinting respects your customers' knowledge and requires new skills on your part to access this knowledge. Blueprinting occurs *before* you step into your lab to begin actual product development. So if unmet customer needs are minimal—or a poor match with your interests—you can avoid squandering enormous resources. If you uncover significant unmet needs, though, you gain the confidence to invest rapidly and heavily in a new product solution.

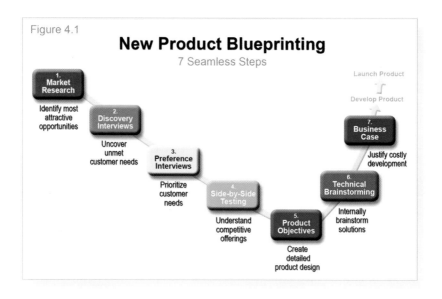

Figure 4.1

New Product Blueprinting

7 Seamless Steps

Seven Blueprinting Steps

When your team uses New Product Blueprinting to design a new product, you move through seven steps (Figure 4.1). First, you conduct *Market Research* to help you segment your markets and ensure you develop products for the most attractive segments. Then you perform a series of *Discovery* (qualitative) and *Preference* (quantitative) Interviews. Now you know what customers really want, but not what competitors are capable of delivering... so you conduct *Side-by-Side Testing*.

Next, your team huddles with all this outside-in data to set its *Product Objectives*. This is what you want to do, but *Technical Brainstorming* is needed to determine what you likely can do. You wrap all this together in a *Business Case* so you can secure the heavy resources needed for the product development and launch phases.

While all seven steps (and their sequence) are important, the centerpiece of New Product Blueprinting is the customer interview. When you interview your customers in a manner expressly designed for intelligent, interested B2B buyers, you come across as caring and competent. That not only opens the door to great new product designs, but marks you as a supplier with whom they'll want to do business.

Seven Steps of New Product Blueprinting

Step 1: Market Research. Beautiful product development in an ugly market segment makes no sense, so sift your potential opportunities early and cheaply. You do this with internet-based market research, combined with simple but effective screening tools.

Step 2: Discovery Interviews. Technical-commercial teams interview customers using qualitative techniques to uncover dozens of needs in depth. You enter the customer's world to discover and understand what will excite *him*.

Step 3: Preference Interviews. In a second round of interviews, you quantitatively prioritize customer needs that are most important and least satisfied. You replace your internal bias with hard data… and kill your project if customers aren't *eager* for change.

Step 4: Side-by-Side Testing. You compare existing products you may have with your competitors' best. This baseline helps you attack their weak spots, avoid getting blind-sided, and optimize pricing… possible only when you understand all your customers' options.

Step 5: Product Objectives. You now have a wealth of outside-in customer and competitive data. Your project team uses this data to create a blockbuster product design in which specific customer needs are targeted and market reaction predicted.

Step 6: Technical Brainstorming. You've got the "what" (your product design), but must now consider the "how"… preliminary technical paths to pursue. This brainstorming includes technical solutions that come from outside as well as inside your company.

Step 7: Business Case. Would a venture capitalist fund your project? Twelve points must be addressed in every Blueprinting project. This drives out assumptions, bias, omission and wishful thinking *before* you begin heavy spending in the product development stage.

Is This Too Much Work?

Does this seem like a lot of work? Seven steps before you even begin the actual product development stage? Consider three things: First, you apply the full process only to major new product initiatives. For smaller projects, individual steps are often used as appropriate. (Once learned, a new mind-set also trickles down to smaller projects: Teams question whether customer needs have been fully explored and competitive positions understood.)

Second, over 35 years of independent research in product development points to one screaming headline: "We're doing terrible up-front work!"[1] This is the subject of Chapter 6, but in more than 30 years of personal B2B experience I have never heard someone say, "Yeah… we sure did too much homework on *that* new product."

Third, rushing through the front end of new product development seldom saves a producer time and money. Quite the contrary. As the auto mechanic in an oil filter commercial used to say, "You can pay me now or you can pay me later," referring to the high price of engine repairs. Rather than *adding* resources to handle front-end work, think of *shifting* resources up and out. Move them "up" in time by shifting some resources from the costly product development stage to the front end of the process. Move them "out" by talking less to yourselves internally and more with customers.

> Our advice to commercial people is "search now, sell later." For technical people, "search now, solve later."

Search Now... Sell and Solve Later

New Product Blueprinting calls for new approaches not only in *how* you interview customers, but in *what* you discuss with them. When most B2B suppliers call on their customers, they are doing one of two things: selling or solving. The sales and marketing people are peddling their wares, and the technical people are fixing whatever is broken. For Blueprinting interviews, our advice to commercial people is "search now, sell later." For technical people, "search now, solve later."

For these interviews, you are interested only in the results customers desire. Customers don't give a hoot about your products… they just want certain things to happen for *them*. When you're selling your ideas, customers know you're not all that interested in them. When you're solving problems with them, you're jeopardizing your intellectual property. In both cases, you're wasting precious customer face time instead of probing to understand how you can deliver value competitors are missing.

Figure 4.2

Ever Lead with *Your* Solution?

Meet your architect…

This is the house for you. Want to talk about it?

I created this design, and it's all I sell. You like it?

You can use this concept to stand out from your competitors… many of whom behave like the architect in Figure 4.2. How would you feel if your architect met with you, showed you his design and said, "I created this design, and it's all I sell. You like it?" And yet this is the treatment many B2B customers get from their suppliers.

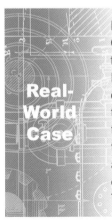

Real-World Case

I accompanied a client on his first Discovery Interview. On the drive there, I was told this prospect had a reputation for being "really tough on suppliers." Wonderful, I thought. True to form, the customers' Executive VP opened the meeting with a few stiff remarks and all the wrong body language. But 10 minutes into the interview, he was completely engaged, later inviting us to lunch and a plant tour. At the end, he leaned back and said, "This has been truly *refreshing*. All our other suppliers come here and try to sell us something. You're the first one who asked us *what we wanted*."

It's All About Customer Outcomes

For the rest of this book, we will use the term "outcome" to refer to a *result the customer desires*. (We highly recommend Tony Ulwick's ground-breaking book, *What Customers Want*, for a thorough discussion of this subject.[2]) New Product Blueprinting gives you great insight into customer outcomes: You measure an *outcome's* importance to customers, gauge current customer satisfaction with *outcomes*, test competitors' ability to satisfy *outcomes*, and create a new product design around key *outcomes*. But first, you must be able to easily identify an outcome when you hear it in an interview. For our purposes, you know you've heard an outcome when three conditions are met:

1) It has obvious, intrinsic customer value.
2) It is usually stable over time.[3]
3) It is independent of any specific solution.

Have you ever heard someone say, "Don't ask customers what they want... they never asked for a microwave oven or CAT scan machine." True, but these are *solutions*. We'll have more success asking customers about desired *outcomes* instead. Imagine you were interviewing health care professionals as part of your up-front work to develop a CAT scan machine. Would it not be helpful to learn about the outcomes shown in Figure 4.3?

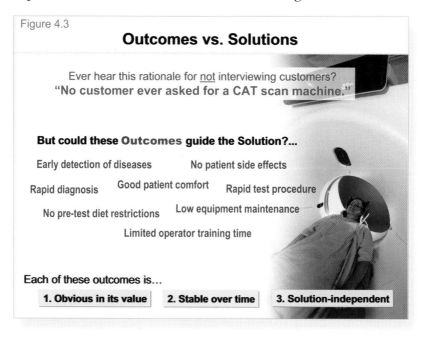

Figure 4.3

Outcomes vs. Solutions

Ever hear this rationale for <u>not</u> interviewing customers?
"No customer ever asked for a CAT scan machine."

But could these Outcomes guide the Solution?...

Early detection of diseases   No patient side effects

Rapid diagnosis   Good patient comfort   Rapid test procedure

No pre-test diet restrictions   Low equipment maintenance

Limited operator training time

Each of these outcomes is...

| 1. Obvious in its value | 2. Stable over time | 3. Solution-independent |

Most companies either bring their own solutions to the customer meeting, or they try to figure out the solutions during the customer meeting. But a solution is nothing more than *one* possible way of satisfying a customer outcome. It may be the best way… but often is not. New Product Blueprinting practitioners apply new listening and probing skills designed to understand each outcome to its fullest. After these outcomes are understood and quantitatively prioritized, there is plenty of time for the supplier to privately develop solutions and build an intellectual property hedge around them.

Think of it this way: Breakthroughs occur when an important and unsatisfied outcome meets a qualified solution. The outcomes are usually known (if poorly articulated) by the customer, and the solutions are often available to the supplier (with some external searching). So we have two choices: 1) Usher the customer into the supplier's "solution space," or 2) move the supplier into the customer's "outcome space." If you are a supplier bent on growth from profitable, protected products, you *must* go for Door #2.

New Product Blueprinting uncovers and "processes" customer outcomes. It's like the business of mining and refining gold ore (Figure 4.4). Market segmentation helps you dig only where rich deposits of gold lie. With Discovery and Preference Interviews, you scoop up as many outcomes as possible and then sift away the dirt and rubble. You use side-by-side testing

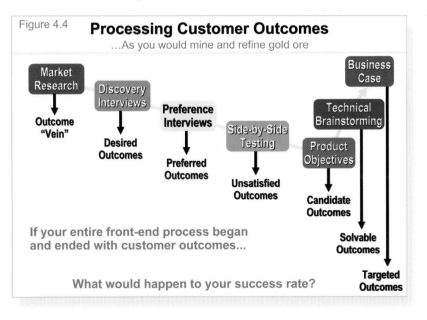

Figure 4.4   Processing Customer Outcomes
…As you would mine and refine gold ore

Market Research → Outcome "Vein"

Discovery Interviews → Desired Outcomes

Preference Interviews → Preferred Outcomes

Side-by-Side Testing → Unsatisfied Outcomes

Technical Brainstorming

Product Objectives → Candidate Outcomes

Business Case

Solvable Outcomes

Targeted Outcomes

If your entire front-end process began and ended with customer outcomes…

What would happen to your success rate?

New Product Blueprinting: What's Different?

Some aspects of New Product Blueprinting are drawn from earlier methodologies, such as traditional Voice of the Customer, Quality Function Deployment and Design for Six Sigma. But our exclusive focus on B2B allows—even demands—that many elements be completely new for maximum effectiveness. A brief summary of 12 key differences is provided here to help you put New Product Blueprinting in perspective:

1. Front-End Scope. While many VOC methods focus primarily on interviews, we cover the entire front end of new product development with interlocking steps. Sometimes New Product Blueprinting is used with a company's existing stage-and-gate process; in other cases it becomes a stand-alone remedy to the problematic "fuzzy front end."

2. Market Segmentation. Our first step is to analyze market segments. Many processes skip this and waste resources on segments that are either unwinnable or not worth winning. In later steps, we use quantitative interview data to fine-tune which customers truly belong in the target market segment before continuing.

3. Customer-Directed Interviews. B2B interviewees are experienced professionals, so we don't approach them with cleverly-scripted questionnaires. Instead we ask simple questions that encourage them to direct us to the areas *they* are most concerned with… all within our project scope, of course.

4. Digital Projection. Displaying interviewees' responses on a screen may seem minor, but it is not. It promotes a respectful peer-to-peer dialogue, creates an "idea-generation" atmosphere, allows real-time corrections, and makes the customer feel much more engaged.

5. No Solutions, No Selling. Our probing questions keep leading us to customers' desired outcomes. We're intentional about staying clear of solutions (which wastes time and jeopardizes intellectual property) and selling (which wastes time and appears self-serving).

6. Minimal Interview Debriefing. VOC interviews that call for tape-recording require hours of transcribing and interpretation. Our B2B customers are capable—and usually eager—to help us understand their comments and prioritize needs while they're still in the room with us.

7. Competitive Testing Linked to Interviews. Instead of huddling internally to develop test procedures—using House of Quality, for instance—our interview questions let *customers* help us design this testing... greatly improving its relevance and customer engagement.

8. Crystal-Clear Product Design. After interviews and competitive testing, the project team uses several "outside-in" graphics to set product objectives. Visual tools help them view "what-if" product designs, predict market reaction to each, and select their preferred design.

9. Technical Brainstorming. Many companies start product development with internal idea generation. We wait to focus brainstorming on outcomes customers really care about. We also tap into experts outside the company and use web-based tools for global collaboration.

10. Business Case. This is much more than a review created for management. It is a living document built at every step of a team's front-end work...so the *team* can plan an exciting project or kill an undeserving one. It's packed full of hard customer and competitor data to eliminate assumptions and internal bias.

11. Building Corporate Memory. Instead of using many unconnected tools, we capture the entire front-end of product development in a single Excel document. This gives teams an easy-to-follow road map and builds corporate memory by allowing easy data retrieval later.

12. Designed for the Masses. We're not keen on having just a few internal experts hear your customers' "voice." We use workshops, coaching and follow-up so a critical mass of your organization is uncovering customer needs and becoming less internally-focused. We don't feel you should outsource this work to VOC consultants... it's a strong competitive competency *you* should build.

to focus on those outcomes not being satisfied by other suppliers. This lets your team select a set of candidate outcomes and then see which will likely be solvable. These are the outcomes you target in your business case, pursue during development, and promote heavily during launch.

New Skills and Tools Needed

New Product Blueprinting calls for a major reversal from the solutions-leading approach most suppliers use. I would like to say you can pull it off with the same set of skills and tools now in place, but it just isn't so. While most traditional voice-of-the-customer (VOC) approaches involve the development of lengthy interview guides, our questions are few and quite simple.

Instead of training practitioners how to develop brilliant questions, we train them to brilliantly probe customer responses. At first this can be unsettling because you have no idea where the customer will take you. How much more comfortable and predictable to fill in the answer to question #17 and then move on to #18. In fact, none of us is smart enough to think of all the right questions before a B2B interview. That's why we need to follow the customer's lead *during* the interview.

> Instead of training practitioners how to develop brilliant questions, we train them to brilliantly probe customer responses.

Fortunately, these skills can be learned in a few days and then finely honed over time. Over and over, our clients find the first couple of interviews to be "different," but successful. They hear things they never heard, get positive customer reactions and then start to really enjoy the process. To our knowledge, none of our clients has ever "gone back" to traditional VOC methods after using this approach. After all, once the skills are learned, preparation time is shorter, hours of post-interview transcribing are eliminated, customers are impressed... and more of the "good stuff" is uncovered.

Moreover, the approach is simple enough to be used by "the masses"—not just a handful of highly-trained VOC experts within your company. When you have large numbers of these customer interviews routinely occurring throughout your business, you gain an enormous competitive edge. This widespread and consistent use of an outside-in, best-practice process is what New Product Blueprinting is all about.

That's it for Part I. I hope you appreciate the uniqueness—and advantages—of B2B vs. consumer goods, aspire to be a builder who maximizes profits, and grasp the essentials of New Product Blueprinting. Now, let's explore the five principles that under-gird Blueprinting.

Endnotes

1. Robert G. Cooper, *Winning at New Products*, 2nd Edition (Reading, Mass: Addison-Wesley, 1993), 22. Dr. Cooper cites the work of D. S. Hopkins and E. L. Bailey ("New Product Pressures," Conference Board Record 8, pp 16-24) in which inadequate market analysis was found to be the leading cause of new product failure—by far, at 45%. The study was reported in 1971. In his 3rd edition by the same name (page 401, endnotes), Dr. Cooper cites several studies that examine new product success and failure going back to the 1970's and concludes, "...but the reasons remain much the same!"

2. Anthony W. Ulwick, *What Customers Want* (New York: McGraw-Hill, 2005). Ulwick's work, in our view, is some of the most innovative in the field of innovation today. We are indebted in particular to his development of the *outcome statement*, which is discussed in Chapter 11. This has allowed Blueprinting practitioners to add a higher level of rigor to their Discovery Interview probing.

3. Some companies worry that their customers' needs will have changed by the time their product is launched. That can easily happen if they target specific solutions that seem reasonable at the time, without understanding customers' underlying desired outcomes. Ulwick has observed that true outcomes usually remain stable over several years. See Anthony W. Ulwick, *What Customers Want* (New York: McGraw-Hill, 2005), 52.

Part I: Overview

Chapter

1. This Book Is for B2B... Not Consumer Goods
2. This Book Is for Builders... Not Decorators
3. This Book Is for Maximizing Profits
4. What Is New Product Blueprinting?

Part II: Five Principles

5. Principle 1: Avoid Incrementalism and Its Death Spiral
6. Principle 2: Upgrade Your New-Product Machine
7. Principle 3: Pick Your Battleground Markets Wisely
8. Principle 4: Use Customer Interviews for a Competitive Edge
9. Principle 5: Develop Your People... Transform Your Business

Part III: Seven Steps

10. Step 1: Market Research
11. Step 2: Discovery Interviews
12. Step 3: Preference Interviews
13. Step 4: Side-by-Side Testing
14. Step 5: Product Objectives
15. Step 6: Technical Brainstorming
16. Step 7: Business Case

Part II

Part II covers five important foundational principles. Think of this section as the "why" and Part III as the "how." This isn't an academic exercise: Unless busy employees appreciate the "why," few bother with the "how."

Chapter 5

Principle 1: Avoid Incrementalism and Its Death Spiral

The Risk Paradox
The Death Spiral
Incrementalism in a Global Economy
"Great Hope" Projects
We Need to "Get Out" More
Moving from Incremental to Breakthrough

When a company relies heavily on new product "tweaks"—offering scant value to customers—the downward spiral doesn't always lead to its death. Often the condition is more akin to life support. The business still exists, but is marginalized and powerless within its industry. In either case, the end result is often irreversible, usually predictable and always unpleasant.

The Risk Paradox

Some producers incrementalize because they don't appreciate how risky this behavior is. Imagine two scenarios. In the first, you've been asked to lead a new product development team. Your team could either make mi-

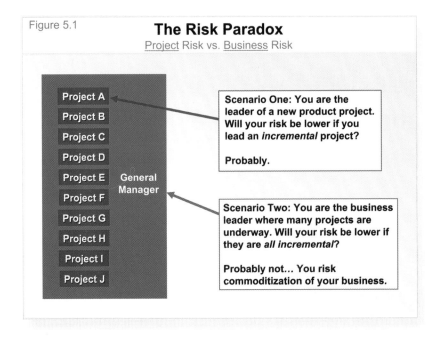

Figure 5.1

The Risk Paradox
Project Risk vs. Business Risk

Scenario One: You are the leader of a new product project. Will your risk be lower if you lead an *incremental* project?

Probably.

Scenario Two: You are the business leader where many projects are underway. Will your risk be lower if they are *all incremental*?

Probably not... You risk commoditization of your business.

nor modifications to an existing product… or attempt a blockbuster based on new technology. Which do you choose? If you want to minimize your risk—work on easy targets now and avoid an inquisition later—chances are you'll start tweaking.

In the second scenario, you've been promoted to general manager over this business, which has several new product projects in the works: A-J in Figure 5.1. Here's the question: To minimize your risk, should all of the projects be low-risk, new product tweaks? No. This is the Risk Paradox: *A business that relies on low-risk, incremental new products is at great risk.*

The Death Spiral

Let's think about what happens when you simply crank out new products that look like your existing products. Over time, your products also begin looking like your competitors' products. Since your customers' purchasing agents didn't just fall off the turnip wagon, they move to commoditize your products. They deem the products they buy to be interchangeable and force you to drop your price... lest they "interchange" you out of the picture.

Now it is time to budget for next year. Declining prices have led to declining profits, and nothing in your new product pipeline will change this anytime soon. Do you hand your boss a budget that promises reduced profits next year, with the cheerful notion that he can expect more of the same in following years? I'm guessing… no.

The Risk Paradox: A business that relies on low-risk, incremental new products is at great risk.

You have two choices: 1) "Buy" market share by dropping your prices, hoping competitors won't match you, or 2) reduce your costs. Since the first approach can turn ugly very quickly, you opt to reduce costs. But what costs to reduce? Surely nothing that's going to hurt business in the near-term.

How about R&D? After all, we're not really sure what these people do anyway, right? So if you cut some R&D costs and meet your budget next year, where are you then? Year by year, your capacity for pulling out of the death spiral diminishes, as your resources to produce differentiated new products are reduced. At some point, the spiral can become irreversible. Sadly, more than a few companies have reached this point.

Incrementalism in a Global Economy

Some time ago, a popular notion claimed companies could be equally successful with a strategy of customer intimacy, operational efficiency or product innovation. Pick a strategy, any strategy. And it was common to hear business leaders in highly-developed economies say their goal was to be the low-cost leader. And why not? Someone within that national economy had to be the low-cost leader, right?

Of course, the boundaries for many of these economies have been rapidly stretched from national to global. As many producers in developed regions have learned to their chagrin, new offshore competitors can have *much* lower cost structures than they. Trying to compete with them on the basis of cost is a bit like taking a knife to a gun fight. Likewise, customer intimacy will take you only so far. Your customers may like you—a lot—but if global competition is also threatening their survival, they will buy from an offshore competitor in a heartbeat. And even if they are not at risk, your customer intimacy is seldom a source of *sustainable* competitive advantage, as key company players come and go.

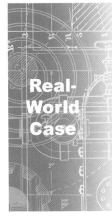

On one ride home from the airport, I asked the driver how long he had been driving cabs. He said off and on for several years… but mostly when his business wasn't going well. Of course, since he was driving at that point, I was curious about his business. He said that his wide-format printing business had just lost two $30,000 jobs for printing trade show graphics. His long-time clients took their business to a Chinese printer… who had bid $6,000!

That leaves us with product innovation. This continues to be the greatest competitive strength for producers in highly-developed economies. Most developing economies follow the model of 1) imitate, 2) improve, and then 3) innovate. But this won't happen at the same pace as it did for Japan. China and other emerging economies are climbing the technology ladder at a phenomenal pace.[1] Bottom line: Unless you are assured of a low-cost position, product incrementalism in a global economy can turn your death spiral into a death plummet.

"Great Hope" Projects

Many companies understand this spiral and want nothing to do with it. So they make sure they have a few "Great Hope" projects. Now these are *big* R&D projects. A team is charged with delivering a product or platform of products that *would* be truly exciting. Their chance of technical success is extremely low, but they don't fully appreciate this because they are charting unknown technical terrain. Since the rest of the company's portfolio is full of incremental projects, no one wants to kill these big projects and be seen as short-sighted or impatient.

The problem with Great Hope projects is that they often fail. Most seasoned executives have had bad experiences with these black holes. They can absorb millions of dollars, tie up valuable resources, divert management attention for two-to-three years and end with a whimper... usually from a fatal flaw that should have been found *much* earlier. Sadly, many businesses fall back into offering incremental new products precisely because of these bad experiences.

We Need to "Get Out" More

So, if both incrementalism and "Great Hope" projects are too risky, what is the answer? I believe we need to "get out" more. Most companies are too internally focused when it comes to understanding two keys areas: customer needs and technical solutions. To put it another way, most companies fail to reduce commercial risk and technical risk because the *knowledge that could reduce their risk resides chiefly outside their company*. As a company shifts from an internal to an external viewpoint, assumptions are tested and options are multiplied. These are great ways to reduce risk, but they won't happen much *inside* your company (Figure 5.2).

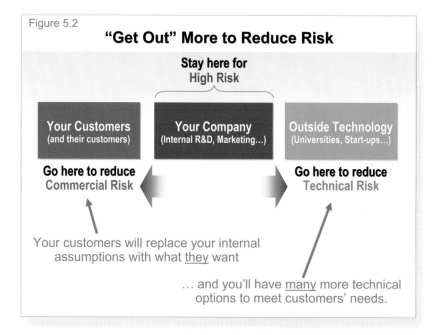

Figure 5.2

"Get Out" More to Reduce Risk

You can reduce *commercial risk* in two ways when you conduct B2B customer interviews. First, as you enter your customers' world through in-depth interviews and tours, you'll discover needs others have missed... so your new product can make customers grin instead of yawn. Second, you'll be able to kill big projects before they start if you find customers aren't interested in *your* "next big thing."

You can reduce *technical risk* by searching for technology that you don't have... but others do. The concept has been dubbed "open innovation" by Henry Chesbrough and is built on the notion that "not all of the smart people work for you." P&G, for instance, set the five-year goal of sourcing 50% of its innovation from the outside, up from 10% in 2002.[2] (More on this in *Step 6: Technical Brainstorming.*)

Moving from Incremental to Breakthrough

When you get out more, you not only reduce risk, you move from incremental to breakthrough products. It is common for companies to focus on incremental products because it is so easy: "We'll just take our existing technology and give customers what they ask for" (Figure 5.3).

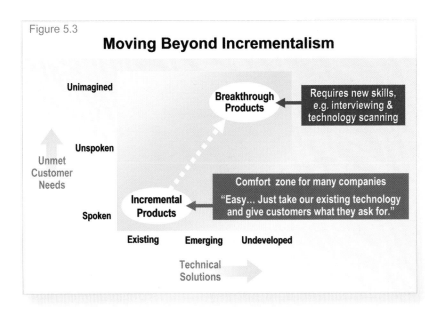

Figure 5.3
Moving Beyond Incrementalism

But when you offer incremental new products, you are in the reactive mode, responding to competitive offerings and customer requests. With break-through new products, you take charge of your destiny. According to Cooper and Kleinschmidt, new products that offer minimal advantage garner 11.6% market share, while those offering high advantage gain 53.5% market share.[3] This is a staggering differential. And with breakthrough products it is much more likely that you will offer novel, non-obvious, useful—and therefore patent-protected—solutions, so attractive profit margins can be maintained longer.

But moving from incremental to breakthrough offerings requires new skills. Your teams need to know how to interview customers in great depth to discover their unspoken and unimagined needs. And when these are uncovered, teams need to be able to reach inside and outside your company for solutions to these unmet needs.

Let's review. Incrementalism puts a business at great risk, but simply investing in large, high-risk projects is not the answer. We need to be more innovative about how we innovate. We need to ask questions that cannot be answered from within our company. We need to ask these questions of our customers (and often their customers) to understand their unmet needs and reduce our commercial risks. And we need to ask these questions of external technologists to find novel solutions that reduce our technical risks. As we adopt these risk-reducing behaviors, paradoxically, we offer more—not less—exciting products to customers.

Endnotes

1. Oded Shenkar, *The Chinese Century* (Upper Saddle River, NJ: Wharton School Publishing, 2005), 2-3. In many labor-intensive industries, e.g. toys, bicycles and shoes, China produces more than half of the world's products. But its global market share is growing rapidly in higher-tech products as well: "The country builds half of the world's microwave ovens, one-third of its television sets and air conditioners, a quarter of its washers, and one-fifth of its refrigerators; these products represent the fastest-growing segment of its exports."
2. Henry W. Chesbrough, *Open Innovation* (Boston: Harvard Business School Press, 2003).
3. Robert G. Cooper, *Winning at New Product, 3rd Edition* (Reading, Mass: Perseus Books, 2001), 58.

Chapter 6

Principle 2: Upgrade Your New-Product Machine

The New-Product Machine
Five Front-End Valuation Errors
Pay Attention to the Front End
Benefits to Upgrading the Front End

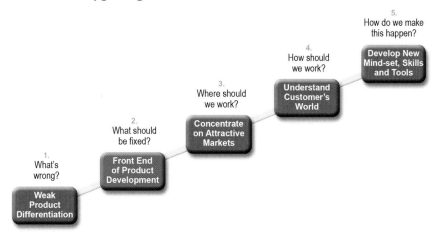

Ever watch a chess game in which one opponent realized the game was over before the other? The loser kept moving his pieces, not realizing the critical moment had passed and defeat was inevitable. Sadly, many companies invest most of their new product development resources *after* the game is over. They spend generously in the development stage, but their product was doomed by earlier, ill-conceived "moves." To appreciate this, consider two processes. Each has identifiable inputs, operations and outputs, so think of these processes as "machines" to be studied and improved.

The New-Product Machine

Most manufacturing companies have two product machines: The "old-product machine" makes products you *know* customers want, while the

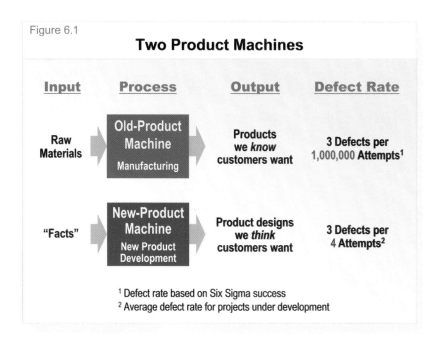

Figure 6.1

Two Product Machines

Input	Process	Output	Defect Rate
Raw Materials	**Old-Product Machine** Manufacturing	Products we *know* customers want	3 Defects per 1,000,000 Attempts[1]
"Facts"	**New-Product Machine** New Product Development	Product designs we *think* customers want	3 Defects per 4 Attempts[2]

[1] Defect rate based on Six Sigma success
[2] Average defect rate for projects under development

"new-product machine" makes product designs you *think* customers want (Figure 6.1). The old-product machine is the manufacturing process. You can call its output "old" simply because you've made these products for customers before. The new-product machine is the new product development process. Its output is less tangible but at least as critical: a product *design* that is attractive to customers and profitable to the supplier. The two machines are linked: Output from the new-product machine (product design) establishes the specifications for the old-product machine (production).

The old-product machine is a decent machine. After a great deal of attention by management and employees with belts of various colors, some companies have had impressive Six Sigma success, producing about three defects per *million* attempts. Then there is the new-product machine. Some research shows that only one in four projects becomes a commercial success after the decision has been made to enter the costly development stage.[1]

So this machine is producing three defects per *four* attempts. (And the attempts are serious, since most companies now conduct gate reviews prior to the development stage.[2]) These defects squander immense R&D and commercial resources, as well as fill up the old-product machine's capacity in making low-margin output. In other words, nearly every facet of the company—R&D, marketing, sales and manufacturing—is affected. Imagine this: You sit on the executive team of your company and each functional leader is giving a status report. The head of manufacturing has just reported that defects are now occurring at Six Sigma rates: three out of one million attempts. You're the head of R&D and get to report that your new product defect rate is three out of four attempts. Can you think of any other function within the company where this level of waste is tolerated?

To be fair, the new-product machine has a more difficult assignment. Just as we prize an original painting over a reprint—because we recognize the creativity and effort required—so we appreciate the challenge of developing a winning new product design. We measure old-product

> **You're the head of R&D and get to report that your new product defect rate is three out of four attempts.**

machine success with the question, "Is the output the same?" while we ask of the new-product machine, "Is the output different—and better?" Also, because the new-product machine deals in intangibles, we find its variables much more difficult to measure and control.

But can we do no better? Your Chief Technology Officer may never have Three or Four Sigma celebrations, but there is more latent corporate value that can be unlocked here than anywhere else. Consider the millions or billions your company invests in R&D during development and in commercial resources during product launch. Imagine the impact highly successful new products would have on employees… on competitors… on investors. This could change the very nature of your company.

So, how many of these defects are part and parcel of new product development, and how many can be driven out—in much the way variability is relentlessly hunted in the old-product machine? Fortunately, we have known for some time which parts of the new-product machine are malfunctioning, and we even know some of the upgrades that will help. Let's look at the malfunctions first.

Five Front-End Valuation Errors

Imagine you are at a review meeting trying to decide if a project should enter the development stage. You are about to make a valuation—an estimation of something's worth—weighing the likely benefits of this project against its costs. My "golden rule" of valuation is: *Make your decision when you've gathered the most facts and spent the least money.* Since pre-development activities are expressly designed for gathering facts, and most companies make at least 90% of their project investment after this point,[3] you are at the right meeting. So far, so good.

> Golden Rule of Valuation: Make your decision when you've gathered the most facts and spent the least money.

You and your colleagues must now avoid five types of valuation errors (Figure 6.2). Understanding these errors will help you make a better valuation of the project at this meeting. More importantly, this understanding can help your company's teams avoid valuation errors *before* such meetings. After all, having good project reviews is a little like having good quality inspectors at the end of a production line. While inspection is useful, we have learned from Dr. Deming that it is much better to understand root problems and provide teams with tools and skills to overcome them.[4] The same can be said for upgrading the new-product machine.

Figure 6.2

Five Valuation Errors

Error	Leading Cause
Type 1 Poorly Analyzed Facts	A disciplined process is lacking
Type 2 Wrong Facts	Untested assumptions are accepted
Type 3 Missing Facts	Key questions are never asked
Type 4 Misinterpreted Facts	Insufficient expert challenging occurs
Type 5 Undiscovered Facts	Probing skills & tools are lacking

Each of these valuation errors concerns the *facts* that should have been addressed before entering the development stage. In our new-product machine metaphor, think of facts as the raw material we feed into the machine. Problems arise when these facts are 1) poorly analyzed, 2) wrong, 3) missing, 4) misinterpreted or 5) undiscovered. Substandard raw material invariably leads to defective output. In the case of the new-product machine, defective output is a product design that fails to impress the customer and enrich the supplier.

1. Poorly Analyzed Facts. This occurs when projects are not consistently evaluated using criteria that reflect your company's true goals. Perhaps you are using the wrong metrics, weightings or financial measures. Maybe an ill-conceived project is funded simply because it is a favorite of top management. Settle on the right criteria and require their even-handed use for all projects. But don't let this become a major internal exercise: Some companies spend too much time building sophisticated analysis models when the "facts" themselves were in desperate need of correction or replacement. I have never traced the cause of a new product flop to using the wrong discount rate in a financial model, for instance. Bottom line: This is often the least critical of the five fact errors, so don't spend all of your time on analysis models.

2. Wrong "Facts." Wrong facts can come from a faulty market research report or miscalculations, but these are minor compared to the main source: untested assumptions. It all starts innocently enough. Someone *thinks* customers make their buying decision this way, *thinks* competitors don't have that technology, and so forth. The thinkers are not motivated to prove their thinking was wrong, others are too busy to do so, and these assumptions take on the appearance of proven facts with each passing meeting. Hard to correct this? Not at all. *Require* facts and assumptions to be clearly labeled as one or the other... and those characterized as facts to be supported by external sources.

> *Require* facts and assumptions to be clearly labeled as one or the other... and those characterized as facts to be supported by external sources.

3. Missing Facts. The third valuation error type occurs when key questions that should have been answered were not. Of course, the overwhelming reason they were not answered is that they were never asked. Perhaps you did not ask about an alternate solution available to customers based on a totally different technology from your product. Or maybe you never considered a regulatory roadblock or some other "showstopper" and its early warning signs. A checklist at a project review can catch many of these, but it is not the most efficient approach. Instead, have teams prepare a business case to be reviewed prior to beginning the development stage. Team members should know all the key business case questions as they *begin* their up-front work: The business case should be more of an operating manual than a mid-term exam.

> The business case should be more of an operating manual than a mid-term exam.

To develop a strong business case template, we have studied the decision-making processes used by venture capitalists.[5] Through this and years of refinement, we developed a 12-point business case template, which will be discussed in greater detail in Chapter 16. For now, Figure 6.3 provides an example of questions used to avoid "missing facts" for one of the 12 business case points, Value Proposition.

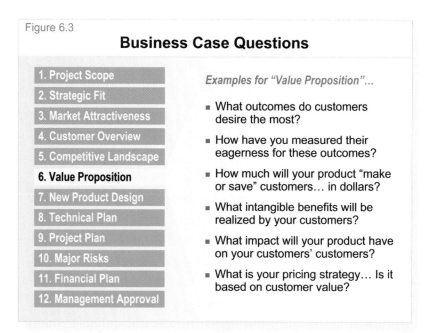

Figure 6.3

Business Case Questions

1. Project Scope
2. Strategic Fit
3. Market Attractiveness
4. Customer Overview
5. Competitive Landscape
6. Value Proposition
7. New Product Design
8. Technical Plan
9. Project Plan
10. Major Risks
11. Financial Plan
12. Management Approval

Examples for "Value Proposition"...

- What outcomes do customers desire the most?
- How have you measured their eagerness for these outcomes?
- How much will your product "make or save" customers... in dollars?
- What intangible benefits will be realized by your customers?
- What impact will your product have on your customers' customers?
- What is your pricing strategy... Is it based on customer value?

4. Misinterpreted Facts. This may be the most difficult to correct. The facts are right, but their implications are wrong, especially concerning future projections. The most common example is the enthusiastic sales projection, shaped like a hockey-stick and accompanied by, "Of course, we think this is actually *conservative* because…" Or perhaps you knowingly launched your new product as a frontal attack on the market leader's stronghold… and had your head handed to you. The team gained experience, but at great cost to your company. The remedy is the thoughtful challenge, born of good judgment from years of experience. Sprinkle your gate review board—and especially your teams—with seasoned new product development veterans and encourage them to ask tough questions. If these veterans are in scarce supply—a common problem—accelerate your organizational learning with post-launch reviews. Focus on past duds, never criticize or even identify the "guilty," create a Pareto chart of root causes and broadly share what has been learned.

5. Undiscovered Facts. We have saved the best for last. Undiscovered facts are quite different from missing facts. When a fact is missing, you can look back and say, "We really should have done a better job of checking this out." In contrast, undiscovered facts are never prompted by internal check-lists; they are uncovered only by external probing. Maybe you failed to find an unspoken customer need that your new product could have addressed to great advantage. Or perhaps customers had an unimagined need that could have surfaced through in-depth probing by your technical staff—which would have led to a blockbuster new product.

> No one is ever faulted for undiscovered facts, and yet more value is probably missed here than with all other valuation errors combined.

No one is ever faulted for undiscovered facts, and yet more value is probably missed here than with all other valuation errors combined. This happens when suppliers use *their* agenda to interact with customers, instead of an open mind and skillful probing. Since outcomes are usually stable over time, it might be years or decades until a sharp supplier uncovers and satisfies customers' most critical outcomes.

Pay Attention to the Front End

You may have noticed that all the malfunctions discussed so far are located at the front end of the new-product machine. This is not to say that the rest of the machine is working flawlessly. In fact, we suspect that when the severe front-end machine problems are overcome, back-end problems (in product development, trial and launch) will become more evident. But we have known for a long time that something is very wrong with the fuzzy front end. As long ago as the early 1970s, inadequate market analysis was cited as the leading cause of new product failures.[6]

More recently, the American Productivity & Quality Center performed a major product development benchmarking study in which 12 practices were found to be particularly strong drivers of performance, with correlation coefficients of 0.5 to 0.7 for overall new product success and profitability.[7] Six of these practices are completely or largely performed prior to the product development stage.

A good stage-gate® process might help, but there was little evidence for this in the above study.[8] While I applaud the discipline of gate-review processes, I routinely see two pitfalls in how they are implemented. First, teams are often asked good questions at gate reviews but have not been trained how to find the answers. *It's as though the test was given but the teaching had yet to occur.* Second, many such processes are too internally focused. Enormous time can be spent doing business with colleagues in the same company... completing forms, attending meetings, giving presentations, and so forth.

If you want some insight into your company's use of its gate-review process, ask teams these two questions: "Since your last project review, how many person-days did you spend talking about this project with other company employees? And how much time with customers and prospects?" (Don't do this publicly... other than perhaps a distant cricket chirping, it tends to get very quiet.)

Benefits to Upgrading the Front End

So much for new-product machine malfunctions. What about upgrades? As you might guess, they address the front end, they concern the handling of facts, they are outside-in and they require new skills and tools. It is best if these practices are linked, and that's the purpose of New Product Blueprinting: a single methodology that brings clarity to the fuzzy front end.

We know from the research cited earlier that solid up-front work leads to more successful new product development. But how does this happen? There are six results delivered by this up-front work, which can be observed *throughout* the entire product development process. When you get the front end working well, you will:

1) Kill projects faster if you learn real customer needs do not exist.
2) Learn competitors' positions early so you can adjust your attack.
3) Use in-depth customer insights to build stronger value propositions.
4) Accelerate development time with clear, stable product objectives.
5) Learn how to most effectively promote and price your new product.
6) Engage and prime customers to buy your new product

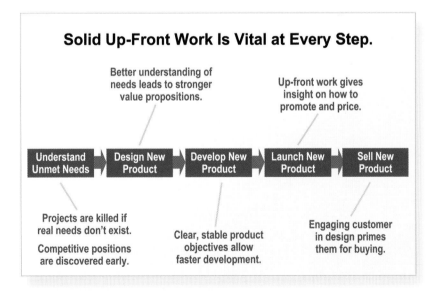

Solid Up-Front Work Is Vital at Every Step.

With all these benefits, you might expect companies would spend a significant portion of their project spending in the front end. In fact, most companies spend less than 10% of a typical project's total cost here.[9] That's unfortunate, because up-front work is not only effective; it is cost-effective. Imagine you have spent $50,000-$100,000 in up-front work... secondary market research reports, travel costs for interviewing customers, competitive lab testing, etc.[10] What would it take to recover these costs? For most projects you will recover your up-front investment if you either...

- Improve probability of new product success by 1%, or
- Increase market share by 1/2 share point, or
- Accelerate time-to-market by 1 month, or
- Raise pricing by 0.5%[11]

In our experience, solid up-front work provides benefits far exceeding these meager break-even levels. And there is great value in up-front work beyond its impact on *successful* projects. Solid up-front work allows companies to quickly kill ill-conceived projects, so that precious resources can be directed to higher-value projects. In too many companies, fuzzy up-front work leads to indecisiveness: Instead of killing projects, they badly wound them.

So why don't businesses do better up-front work? Business leaders inherently understand the value of doing one's homework before starting an im-

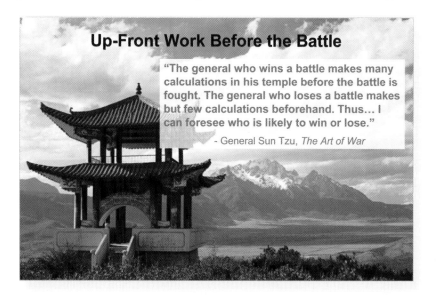

Up-Front Work Before the Battle

"The general who wins a battle makes many calculations in his temple before the battle is fought. The general who loses a battle makes but few calculations beforehand. Thus... I can foresee who is likely to win or lose."

- General Sun Tzu, *The Art of War*

portant task, but often *don't know how* regarding new product development. Or if they do, they are not sure how to implement a transformational change across their entire organization. This is precisely the goal of New Product Blueprinting: Dramatically upgrade the up-front new product work done by B2B producers... do this rapidly and with as little wasted motion as possible... and do this so that the new practices become a permanent part of the company.

Endnotes

1   The success rate of new product *ideas* is much lower than one in four. This is understandable since evaluations have not yet been done, and it is acceptable since serious investments have not yet been made. A more telling—and discouraging—statistic is the one-in-four success rate of new product projects approved for entry into the costly development stage. See Robert G. Cooper, *Winning at New Products, 2nd Edition* (Reading, Mass: Perseus Books, 2001), 9. Also see Clayton M. Christensen and Michael E. Raynor, *The Innovator's Solution*, (Boston: Harvard Business School Press, 2003), 73.

2   Paige Leavitt, ed., *Improving New Product Development Performance and Practices* (Houston: APQC International Benchmarking Clearinghouse, 2003), 18-19.

3   Ibid, 25-26.

4   Dr. Edward Deming's use of statistical process control in the second half of the 20th century forever changed "quality," especially in the manufacture of products (our "old-product machine"). In his teaching, Dr. Deming discouraged a reliance on end-of-the-line inspection and instead encouraged training in new skills for operators on the line.

5   For an overview of venture capital decision-making practices, see: Justin J. Camp, *Venture Capital Due Diligence*. (New York: John Wiley & Sons, 2002).

6   D. S. Hopkins, and E. L. Bailey, *New Product Pressures* (Conference Board Record 8, 1971) 16-24.

7   Paige Leavitt, ed., *Improving New Product Development Performance and Practices* (Houston: APQC International Benchmarking Clearinghouse, 2003), 45-46.

8   The term Stage-gate® was coined by Dr. Robert Cooper and is a registered trademark of the Product Development Institute, Inc. Stage-gate is a process in which project teams perform prescribed work during a "stage" and then must review it with a management team at a "gate" review before proceeding to the next stage. It has been widely practiced since the 1980s and, in my experience, has brought a helpful level of discipline. At the same time, there is some question as to its overall effectiveness. An APQC benchmarking study did not find a significant correlation between the use of such a process and new product success, yet did find such a relationship in 77 other practices: Paige Leavitt, ed., *Improving New Product Development Performance and Practices* (Houston: APQC International Benchmarking Clearinghouse, 2003).

9   Paige Leavitt, ed., *Improving New Product Development Performance and Practices* (Houston: APQC International Benchmarking Clearinghouse, 2003), 25-26.

10   These figures are for illustration purposes only. Major new product projects can require much larger up-front investment than this. But this cost-effectiveness still applies due to the much larger expected impact of the new product.

11   The following assumptions were made for a new product project: $5 million sales/ year after a 3-year ramp-up; $50 million market size; 30% incremental EBITDA margin; 12% weighted average cost of capital; 2 year time-to-market; working capital equal to 20% of sales; terminal value equal to EBITDA times 7.0; development and launch costs of $500 thousand.

Chapter 7

Principle 3: Pick Your Battleground Markets Wisely

Define "Market Segment"
You Have Choices
Strategic Market Segment Portfolios
Market Segmentation "Rules"

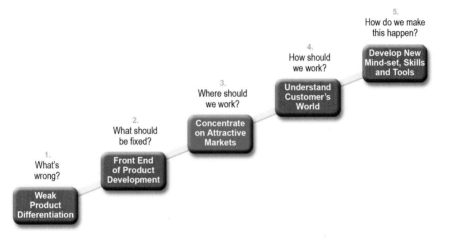

What is the best way to win a war? The military historian Basil Liddell Hart concluded, "All the lessons of war can be reduced to a single word: concentration. But for truth, this needs to be amplified to *the concentration of strength against weakness*."

Can this lesson be applied to business? Imagine the business leader using market research where the general employs reconnaissance, developing a strategic plan instead of a battle plan, and allocating resources instead of deploying troops. Could it be that new product launches and other business initiatives succeed or fail largely due to their level of *concentration*?

Napoleon said, "It is impossible to be too strong at the decisive point." Great military leaders throw the weight of their force at the most important point in the battle front. Losing generals spread their forces thinly, unable to muster an effective attack, remaining on the defensive. In our experience, many business leaders fail to 1) thoroughly understand their battle fronts, 2) determine the decisive points to attack, and 3) follow-through with an overwhelming assault.

Define "Market Segment"

Think of the business leader's potential battle fronts as market segments to pursue. Let's define "market segment." Some companies segment according to their own organizational structure, sales territories, product lines, and so forth. But this is inside-out thinking and flawed. We define a market segment as a *cluster of customers with similar needs.*

For example, suppose your company produces hydraulic cylinders. One market segment for your product might be garbage truck producers, since this cluster of customers has similar needs:

  - Reliability over hundreds of cycles per day
  - Resistance to a broad range of garbage contaminants
  - Low weight for vehicle fuel efficiency
  - Quiet operation for early morning residential use
  - Non-hazardous hydraulic fluid in case of leakage

With good customer interviewing, your list might include over a hundred needs, all common to garbage truck producers. This list would look quite different for other hydraulic cylinder market segments, such as amusement park rides, metal stamping equipment, forklift trucks or earth-moving equipment.

This outside-in approach requires more effort, but is essential. Here's why: Ultimately, everything your business does should be about efficiently delivering value to customers. Now, if you choose any type of segmentation *other* than clustering customers with similar needs, you will not be delivering value efficiently. Different people in your company will learn about market segment needs at different times, under different conditions, at different levels of depth. You will then be forced into one of two paths: 1) Develop new products for one customer at a time, or 2) develop "averaged" products for many dissimilar customers that don't completely satisfy any of them. The former makes you reactive and vulnerable; the latter mediocre.

When you properly cluster customers into market segments, though, you gain tremendous efficiencies. You are able to discriminate between segments, concentrating your troops where it counts. For attractive segments, you can use interviews and other means to understand market needs in far greater depth than competitors. You can collaborate closely with key market players, establishing yourself as a supplier of choice. And you can launch your product with rifle-shot promotional tools aimed at your target market segment. So both "early-stage marketing" (understanding needs) and "late-stage marketing" (promoting solutions) work better. After all, marketing should be about… markets.

> Losing generals spread their forces thinly, unable to muster an effective attack, remaining on the defensive.

You Have Choices

If you are not segmenting your markets by customer clusters today, here's good news: You probably have considerable upside to capture. As we work across a broad range of industries (all B2B), we nearly always find three things to be true: 1) The typical B2B company has many potential segments it *could* serve, 2) these segments vary substantially in their potential for profitable growth, and 3) due to poor segmentation strategy and implementation, enormous value is missed.

It can be tempting to dive into a new product development project without understanding your market… and wrong. Any number of unseen problems could plague you: increasing global competition, smaller-than-expected market size, declining end-use consumer trends, well-entrenched competition, etc. You will eventually learn of these problems, but your cost of doing so could increase one-to-two orders of magnitude if you learn from experience rather than forethought. Ultimately, your market selection sets the ceiling on your new product's potential: You can do the most impressive product development imaginable, but your rewards will be limited if you do it in the wrong market segment.

Many companies do not understand their true "customer clusters" well enough to do full-blown market segmentation initially. That's OK. The idea is to find the *best* points to attack on the battle front and this can take some time. Start where you are with a quick screening of possible segments. (See fictitious example in Figure 7.1.) Gather as much secondary research about each segment as possible so a red-yellow-green "stoplight" assessment can be made. Sure, you could do a more sophisticated analysis with weightings, points and such… but how good is your data until you go *outside* and begin talking to customers?

After you have selected your initial target segment—in the Figure 7.1 example, it might be gym floor coatings—your team will begin its Discovery Interviews, followed by Preference Interviews and the remaining Blueprinting steps. But it is important to stay flexible. At any point in this process, the team should be prepared to drop the market segment opportunity like a hot potato if the segment is found unattractive. The team could then return to this stoplight analysis and move on to the next priority segment.

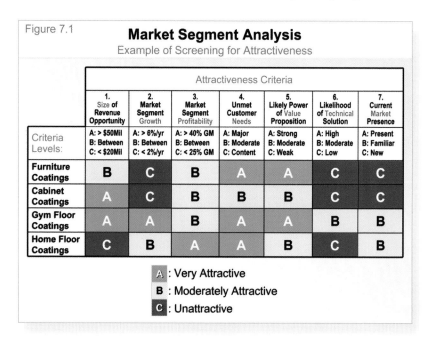

Figure 7.1

Market Segment Analysis
Example of Screening for Attractiveness

	Attractiveness Criteria						
	1. Size of Revenue Opportunity	2. Market Segment Growth	3. Market Segment Profitability	4. Unmet Customer Needs	5. Likely Power of Value Proposition	6. Likelihood of Technical Solution	7. Current Market Presence
Criteria Levels:	A: > $50Mil B: Between C: < $20Mil	A: > 6%/yr B: Between C: < 2%/yr	A: > 40% GM B: Between C: < 25% GM	A: Major B: Moderate C: Content	A: Strong B: Moderate C: Weak	A: High B: Moderate C: Low	A: Present B: Familiar C: New
Furniture Coatings	B	C	B	A	A	C	C
Cabinet Coatings	A	C	B	B	B	C	C
Gym Floor Coatings	A	A	B	A	A	B	B
Home Floor Coatings	C	B	A	A	B	C	B

A : Very Attractive
B : Moderately Attractive
C : Unattractive

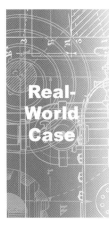

The team had been thinking about pursuing this market segment for over a year. They had talked about it, debated it, and even purchased a fair bit of secondary market research. On their very first Discovery Interview, they were crestfallen to learn that there was absolutely no need for a new product. When we reviewed their progress, my question was, "Did you order pizza and celebrate? Because now you can move on to the next opportunity." Any time you can kill an idea before you enter the costly development stage, you should consider it a victory.

Strategic Market Segment Portfolios

The main objective of New Product Blueprinting is to develop exciting products. There is also another benefit: exciting strategy. Let's briefly look at work you can do that lies *outside* the scope of the seven Blueprinting steps... work that can be aided by first completing the Blueprinting process in several market segments. Your market research, customer interviews and competitive testing put you in a position to perform a *strategic market segment portfolio* analysis. This analysis will be "outside-in" instead of the internal exercises many companies perform.

Figure 7.2 illustrates our preferred approach.[1] In this fictitious example, market attractiveness is driven by segment growth, barriers to entry, rivalry intensity and other characteristics. Competitive position is driven by relative market share, product breadth, cost structure and other factors. You should generally try to improve your competitive position in more attractive segments (moving upper bubbles to the right). But if the "enemy" has amassed his troops at this part of the battle front, you will need to deliver *significant* new product value.

Such a portfolio analysis is typically part of the strategic planning process. It is a powerful way to ensure you aren't "diluting your troops" by spreading them evenly across the battle front. The first time through this analysis, we find most businesses want to "attack" everything. Of course they cannot,

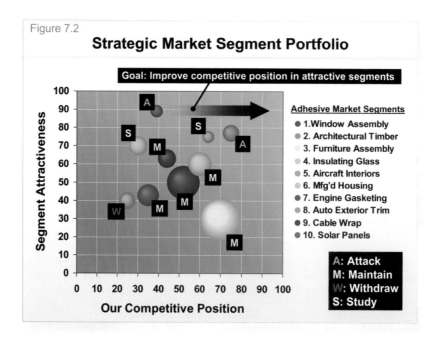

Figure 7.2

Strategic Market Segment Portfolio

Goal: Improve competitive position in attractive segments

Adhesive Market Segments
- 1. Window Assembly
- 2. Architectural Timber
- 3. Furniture Assembly
- 4. Insulating Glass
- 5. Aircraft Interiors
- 6. Mfg'd Housing
- 7. Engine Gasketing
- 8. Auto Exterior Trim
- 9. Cable Wrap
- 10. Solar Panels

A: Attack
M: Maintain
W: Withdraw
S: Study

Segment Attractiveness

Our Competitive Position

and they totally miss the power of *concentration*. Done well, this part of strategic planning allows you to concentrate your troops—usually resources applied toward product development or acquisitions—at the decisive point of the battle.

Market Segmentation "Rules"

It is best to think of market segmentation as a process... not a destination and certainly not an exercise. Here is guidance to consider: First, don't define segments too broadly lest you "average" the needs of customers, and give an opening to competitors who focus more narrowly. Second, organize your business by market segment; many companies begin by establishing market-facing teams that later "morph" into market-facing businesses.

Third, manage segments globally. If there are regional differences in customer needs, you certainly must understand and address these needs *locally* with your new products. But in the new global economy, business can shift rapidly from region to region; highly independent regional organizations create "silos" that hinder global awareness and lead to blind spots.

Finally, once you've completed the analysis shown in Figure 7.2, be *bold* in piling on resources for a limited number of "Attack" segments. Too often I see this part of strategic planning end with a whimper. Your reconnaissance is complete. You have your battle plan. Now it is time to *concentrate* your troops.

Endnotes

1. This approach is rooted in the BCG (Boston Consulting Group) Matrix, in which strategic business units were displayed on a matrix with axes of market growth rate and market share. Later, the GE/McKinsey Matrix expanded the dimension of market growth rate to include other aspects of *market attractiveness*, and market share was recognized as only one dimension of *competitive strength*. Work in this area suggests three elements are often present in a successful business: 1) attractive market, 2) strong competitive position in that market, and 3) a management team that knows what to do with number one and two. In our strategic planning support (typically post-Blueprinting), we help clients apply consistent criteria across many market segments and businesses so that resources can be applied where they will do the most good. Ultimately, any strategic plan that does not result in *change* has largely wasted people's time. The most meaningful change is often reallocating resources: strategic market segment portfolio analysis helps you do this effectively.

Chapter 8

Principle 4: Use Customer Interviews for a Competitive Edge

What Footrace Are You In?
Nothing Comes Close to a Good Interview
Not Your Father's VOC Interview
Search Your Entire Value Chain for Value
Interviewing with a Digital Projector
Theory of Non-Obviousness

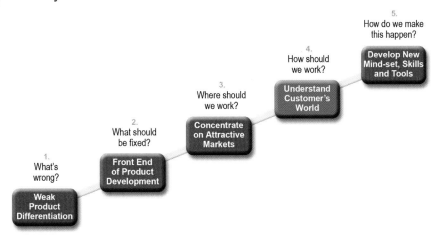

Are you squandering R&D resources? Most companies are. Funny thing is that many corporations already know they are squandering at least half of their millions or billions of R&D dollars. (Studies show companies waste 50-75% of their R&D on unsuccessful new products.[1]) They just don't know which half. Well, actually they do, but not until *after* the money has been spent.

It isn't that their labs are filled with technical people who cannot find the right answers. They are just being asked the wrong questions. Questions that are unimaginative, have been asked at too many other labs, and create too little value if solved. Questions that are too obvious. Let's think about the footrace that takes place as a result.

What Footrace Are You In?

Does this sound familiar? An important customer tells your sales rep what he wants. That starting pistol shot begins the race. Your sales rep hands the request off to R&D, properly packaged and labeled, of course. R&D may ask the rep to go back and ask more questions, but once he has handed off the baton, the sales rep's leg of the relay is pretty much over.

Since the customer is a clever chap, your competitors' sales reps have been given the identical request to drop off at their companies. Terrific. Now you are all in the same footrace, with the customer waiting at the finish line. If you cross the line first, you might get a price premium. But the moment just *one* of your competitors crosses the finish line, you'll hear a giant whooshing sound as all of the value—in the form of pricing—rushes from the suppliers to the customer.

> You'll hear a giant whooshing sound as all of the value—in the form of pricing—rushes from the suppliers to the customer.

What if you ran a different race? This time, you choose the race time and place by targeting an attractive market segment opportunity… which you pursue with in-depth customer interviews. A technical-commercial team uses advanced probing to uncover *unspoken* needs. And since your team knows how to engage the customer in a thought-provoking dialogue, it may also bring back *unimagined* needs. The race is on and your competitors don't know where or when it's being held, or even that a race is being run. The new product you develop is like nothing the customer has seen before—nor will they for a long time if your patents are in order. It delivers real value, which the customer shares with you by paying a fair price premium.

Nothing Comes Close to a Good Interview

That brings us to the subject of this chapter: customer interviews. Of all the ways to learn about customer needs—telephone, mail survey, internet—nothing comes close to face-to-face customer interviews (Figure 8.1).

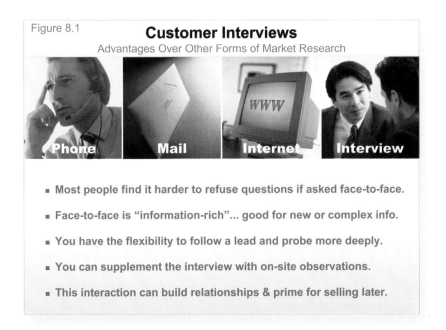

Figure 8.1

Customer Interviews

Advantages Over Other Forms of Market Research

Phone Mail Internet Interview

- Most people find it harder to refuse questions if asked face-to-face.
- Face-to-face is "information-rich"... good for new or complex info.
- You have the flexibility to follow a lead and probe more deeply.
- You can supplement the interview with on-site observations.
- This interaction can build relationships & prime for selling later.

If the information being sought is new, complex or ambiguous—as with B2B product design—the advantages of interviews become even greater.

So is the customer interview a key fixture in most new product development processes? For many producers, the answer is no. Perhaps with so many routine customer interactions, it's assumed much of it *must* be interviewing. But if you examine the call frequency of your sales and technical service staff, you will likely find that over 90% of face-to-face customer communication is of the "tell-and-sell" variety. Some might protest, "But we get lots of input from our customers on what they want in new products." As shown in Figure 8.2, the difference between that and what is being proposed here is the difference of night and day. Most new product discussions are actually customer-reactive meetings, not market-proactive interviews.

You'll know a market-proactive interview when you see it: First, a team targets an attractive market segment. Then it schedules interviews with customers, prospects and their customers' customers. Two-or-three-person technical-commercial teams prepare their questions and interviewing roles in advance. During the interviews, these teams use advanced listening, probing and interviewing skills to plumb incredible depths... and the customers love it!

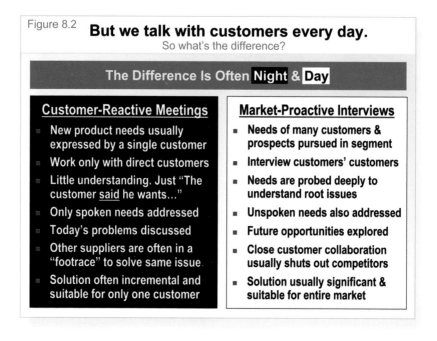

Figure 8.2

But we talk with customers every day.
So what's the difference?

The Difference Is Often Night & Day

Customer-Reactive Meetings	Market-Proactive Interviews
New product needs usually expressed by a single customer	Needs of many customers & prospects pursued in segment
Work only with direct customers	Interview customers' customers
Little understanding. Just "The customer <u>said</u> he wants..."	Needs are probed deeply to understand root issues
Only spoken needs addressed	Unspoken needs also addressed
Today's problems discussed	Future opportunities explored
Other suppliers are often in a "footrace" to solve same issue	Close customer collaboration usually shuts out competitors
Solution often incremental and suitable for only one customer	Solution usually significant & suitable for entire market

Not Your Father's VOC Interview

If a Blueprinting interview is not a customer-reactive sales call, it's also not a traditional VOC (voice-of-the-customer) interview. Please don't get me wrong... I love working with companies that have developed a VOC discipline, be it through quality function deployment, design for Six Sigma or another methodology. After all, these companies are far ahead of most businesses, which use the VOO approach—voice-of-ourselves—also known as "breathing our own fumes."

In fact, New Product Blueprinting was built on the foundation of traditional VOC, and shares a common emphasis on the front end, customer interviews, data-driven decisions, training and multi-functional teams. It's just that New Product Blueprinting is optimized for B2B, and as such, departs significantly in actual practice before, during and after the interview. Here is one example: Traditional VOC interviews are all about asking the *supplier's* questions. Blueprinting interviews center on whatever is important to the *customer...* within the pre-established scope, of course.

Figure 8.3

Q: What should we ask customers about?

A: Whatever is important to them!

Who would <u>you</u> rather have a long conversation with?

**So, let's drop *our* long list of questions…
and discuss what *they* want to see changed.**

Look at the two scenes in Figure 8.3: If you are the customer and have been asked to carve time out of your busy schedule, who would you rather have a long conversation with? If I saw "clipboard guy" coming, I'd get away as fast as I could. Now, if you are doing B2C interviews and *paying* people to respond, this works just fine. But if you are trying to interview customers and prospects on a respectful, peer-to-peer, B2B basis—and hope to engage them in a strong relationship going forward—you *have got* to lose that clipboard.

Real-World Case

Our client's interviewee was clearly not interested in "another interview." She began by looking at her watch and saying, "I can give you 10 minutes." But she became so engaged that the interview lasted an hour and a half. In fact, twice during the interview she tried to take over the job of recording notes: Our client had to fend off her "assaults" on their laptop and projector!

Figure 8.4

Weak Interview Questions

Questions from Actual Interviews ...

Closed-ended question ➤	1. Are you satisfied with your product today?
Looking in rear-view mirror ➤	2. What has helped make your company successful?
Needs are not prioritized ➤	3. What does your customer need in your product?
We've started negotiating ➤	4. What would you be willing to pay for this feature?
Leading the witness ➤	5. Will machines be bigger and faster in the future?
Feels like a "fishing trip" ➤	6. Can you tell us anything about the strategic sourcing initiatives you have?

There are other weaknesses to resolve for the thoughtful B2B interview. Figure 8.4 displays a few actual questions that have been used in traditional interviews and are found lacking. Each of these questions, by itself, does not seem offensive. But taken together, they provide far too little new product direction for the precious customer face-time that has been spent.

Figure 8.5

Why Many Interviews Fall Short

- **Superficial**... Interviewers are untrained in listening & probing skills—so only surface information is gleaned

- **Little Progressive Learning**... Questions are not updated based on knowledge gained in prior interviews

- **Lack of Prioritization**... No means to target highest-impact outcomes from many customers' "laundry lists" of needs

- **Poor Quantification**... No measurement tool to gauge whether customer eagerness is high enough to pursue

- **Difficult to Analyze**... After several such interviews, it is often difficult to sort out common themes and direction

In general, we see the five shortcomings shown in Figure 8.5 arising over and over when companies do try to interview their customers. It would be bad enough if these shortcomings merely hampered the supplier's ability to plan its new product. In addition, though, they allow an enormous opportunity to slip away: the chance to impress the customer or prospect that *they* are the supplier to do business with going forward.

Search Your Entire Value Chain for Value

Perhaps you have a short value chain: You sell fully-assembled beds to hospitals or ingredients to cosmetic companies. In such cases, you are in the B2B world and the principles of this book completely apply. But your value chain is short, because the company you are selling to is the last downstream *company* (since it sells to end consumers).

On the other hand, you may have a longer value chain. Consider Figure 8.6: You sell a resin that your customers use to produce a clear coating. This, in turn, is sold to part manufacturers who spray this coating on automotive exterior parts. These parts are then assembled even further downstream into the final vehicle.

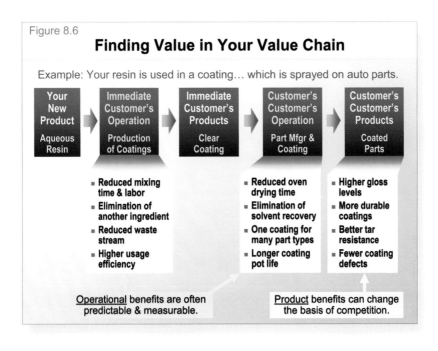

Figure 8.6

Finding Value in Your Value Chain

Example: Your resin is used in a coating... which is sprayed on auto parts.

Should you be satisfied with interviewing just your direct customers... or should you interview *their* customers? In virtually every case, the answer is "go downstream." You might not if your direct customers had complete knowledge of their customers' needs *and* willingly shared it with you. Rarely do both of these conditions occur.

When you interview downstream, you will uncover customer needs that you never dreamed of. And you will stop thinking of your product as a bundle of attributes, and instead as a means for delivering outcomes to the most important players in your value chain. Did you notice that in Figure 8.6, we didn't list any benefits under your aqueous resin, or even your customer's clear coating? That's because these products have absolutely no value in and of themselves. They create value only when used in a downstream *operation* or final *product*. Unless you probe to understand this value through interviews, you will miss critical opportunities to differentiate your product.

A common question is, "But what if my customers don't want me to interview their customers?" In fact, that could be your customers' reaction... but it usually doesn't need to be. We can nearly always eliminate this reaction with some well-planned preemptive moves. While a complete discussion is beyond the scope of this book, one proven method is to remove the fear of the unknown by first interviewing your direct customers. Once they realize this is a positive experience, it is much easier to interview their customers without damaging your relationship with direct customers.

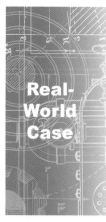

Real-World Case

Our client's product was a component in military equipment that went through a long value chain. In addition to interviewing the customers in the middle of the chain, our client held a Discovery Interview with the governmental department that set the final specifications on the finished military product. At the end of the interview, this department was so impressed that they asked, "We'd like to work with just one supplier on this project... would *you* mind being that supplier?" This gave our client a tremendous advantage in developing their next-generation product.

Interviewing with a Digital Projector

Whether you are interviewing a direct customer or your customer's customer, we recommend letting the customer see everything being recorded. Using a laptop and portable digital projector works well in most cases. (Even if using a projector is impractical, such as at a building site, allow the customer to see the laptop screen.) For Discovery Interviews, customers' ideas are recorded on digital "sticky notes." This adds to the sense they are taking part in a well-planned idea generation process (Figure 8.7).

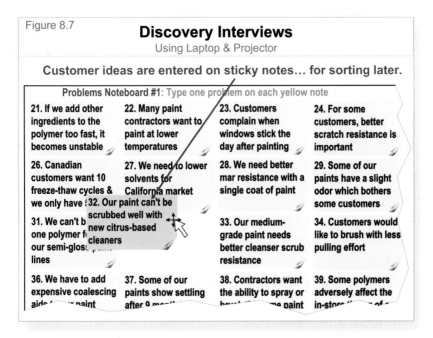

Figure 8.7

Discovery Interviews
Using Laptop & Projector

Customer ideas are entered on sticky notes… for sorting later.

Problems Noteboard #1: Type one problem on each yellow note

21. If we add other ingredients to the polymer too fast, it becomes unstable

22. Many paint contractors want to paint at lower temperatures

23. Customers complain when windows stick the day after painting

24. For some customers, better scratch resistance is important

26. Canadian customers want 10 freeze-thaw cycles & we only have !

27. We need to lower solvents for California market

28. We need better mar resistance with a single coat of paint

29. Some of our paints have a slight odor which bothers some customers

31. We can't b one polymer f our semi-glos: lines

32. Our paint can't be scrubbed well with new citrus-based cleaners

33. Our medium-grade paint needs better cleanser scrub resistance

34. Customers would like to brush with less pulling effort

36. We have to add expensive coalescing aide paint

37. Some of our paints show settling after 9 m

38. Contractors want the ability to spray or paint

39. Some polymers adversely affect the in-store

This approach is so effective because it takes human nature into account. Imagine a supplier is about to interview you in one of three ways. In Scene One, she sits across the desk from you scribbling notes on a notepad as you speak. You have no idea what she is writing, whether she "gets it" or not, or what will become of the notes.

In Scene Two, she conducts the same interview, but is typing notes into her laptop instead. You have the same concerns, but now realize she is creating a digital record you cannot see… that could be sent around the world by the time you finish your coffee. Scene Three is exactly the same as Scene Two with one exception: She has plugged her laptop into a digital projector and everyone in the room is looking at the projection screen together.

Most people have to watch Scene Three to fully appreciate the change that occurs between Scenes Two and Three. Within minutes of the laptop being plugged into the projector, several shifts take place: 1) The customers' attention shifts from the laptop to the projection screen, 2) the dialogue becomes less of an interview and more of a discussion, and 3) the activity feels less like a task or a favor, and more like a team effort. The customers invariably become more engaged, usually give you more time than planned, and often ask for a copy of what you created together. (And since you ventured only into their "outcome space" and not your "solution space," this does not present intellectual-property problems for you.)

Real-World Case

One of our clients was about to interview one of the largest and most sophisticated companies in Germany. This was their first Discovery Interview and they weren't sure the Blueprinting approach would be accepted. The interview was set for 1.5 hours… and lasted 4.5! Their hosts were so excited about the process and what had been accomplished that they asked for another meeting to complete the work. An exception? Not really. We have recorded many interviews in the 4-6 hour range… none of which was ever scheduled to go this long.

There are many benefits to using digital projectors (Figure 8.8). Besides better engagement, customers can make corrections on a real-time basis. This dramatically improves the accuracy of your information. When customers view many ideas at once, it helps them "springboard" off these ideas to new ideas. And you can get customers' help in selecting their best ideas, which can be color-coded, sorted and moved around.

Later, we'll discuss how important it is to have your team debrief immediately after the interview. Your team goes to a nearby restaurant or coffee shop and cleans up its work on the laptop while memories are fresh. This also lets you quickly e-mail the customer a copy of the interview results.

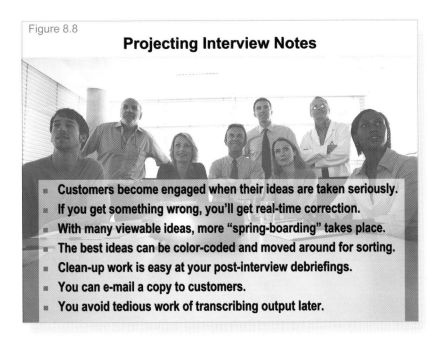

Figure 8.8

Projecting Interview Notes

- Customers become engaged when their ideas are taken seriously.
- If you get something wrong, you'll get real-time correction.
- With many viewable ideas, more "spring-boarding" takes place.
- The best ideas can be color-coded and moved around for sorting.
- Clean-up work is easy at your post-interview debriefings.
- You can e-mail a copy to customers.
- You avoid tedious work of transcribing output later.

Compare this to internal brainstorming sessions you may have attended. Perhaps you ended up with hundreds of sticky notes on a dozen sheets of flip-chart paper. You probably struck fear in the heart of your administrative assistant as you approached with your bazooka-like tube of rolled-up sheets ready for transcribing. This can be *much* easier, and you can engage and impress your customers while you're at it.

That's an overview of Discovery Interviews. We will cover them in detail in Part III, along with Preference Interviews. While *qualitative* Discovery Interviews expand your known universe of customer needs, *quantitative* Preference Interviews tell you which you'll be rewarded for addressing.

If your new product development process does not *require* customer interviews today, consider three questions: 1) How many resources are we wasting by developing products that don't directly address customers' greatest unmet needs? 2) Do we have competitors beating us to the new product punch because they are using traditional interviews to uncover customer needs? 3) Can we leapfrog these competitors by building a new competency in B2B-optimized customer interviews?

Theory of Non-Obviousness

One of the most important goals of a Discovery Interview is to uncover non-obvious customer needs your competitors have missed. Patents are granted only if they are useful, novel and non-obvious. So we already appreciate the value of non-obvious technical solutions. What about the value of non-obvious customer needs? If you'll work through the logic here, you'll see this value can be enormous.

First, imagine your customer has obvious and non-obvious needs and that you can learn about both. If you could pursue any of the four product types shown in Figure 8.9—Me-Too, Long-Shot, Leading or Dominant—which would you target?

Figure 8.9

Four Types of New Products

Like many decisions, it boils down to a question of *risk* and *reward*. In this case, risk is driven by the likelihood you'll find a technical solution. (We said that you can learn about your customers' needs... not necessarily satisfy them.) Reward is largely driven by whether you are the exclusive solution supplier... or one of many suppliers. Let's explore.

In Figure 8.10, the likelihood of technical success increases as you move to the upper-left. Of course, the "likelihood vector" points left because you're using familiar technical solutions. But it also points up because you're trying to answer questions never before asked. The technical answers for these new questions haven't been picked over by other suppliers like the bones of a long-dead wildebeest.

The reward profile (Figure 8.11) is driven by whether you are the exclusive supplier of new customer value. You might price your new

Figure 8.10

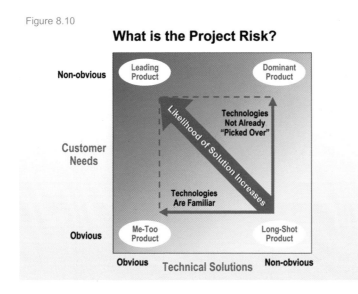

What is the Project Risk?

product to share value 50/50 with your customer. But if a competitor matches your product, you'll be forced to drop your price and most of the value—and your profits—will quickly swing to your customer.

Exclusivity often increases as you move to the right, because your solution is non-obvious and therefore patentable. But the "exclusivity vector" also points up, since you are the first to discover and satisfy a non-obvious need. You'll gain first-mover advantages—branding, industry reputation, learning-curve experience, industry standard-setting, or even an application patent.

Figure 8.11

What is the Project Reward?

Since a project's attractiveness is a combination of its risk and reward, the vectors should be added together, as in Figure 8.12. By pursuing non-obvious needs (the Non-obvious Zone), you'll be the first to uncover important needs. This makes it more likely you'll succeed technically, and gives you first-mover market advantages if you do.

Figure 8.12

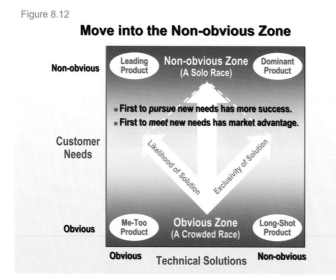

So which projects should you pursue? Most companies can help themselves greatly by spending less time in the Obvious Zone (with obvious needs). It's far too crowded in the realm of the obvious and frankly, it's just plain *hard* to win here. But under the right circumstances, there's room for each project type:

> **Me-Too**: These won't bring you much value, but some may be needed to fill out your product line.
> **Long-Shot**: While these can be a resource sink-hole, they may be worthwhile if you already have a likely technical solution.
> **Leading**: Usually your first line of attack. Move off this only if you can't uncover non-obvious needs or an obvious technical solution.
> **Dominant**: Blockbuster value, but don't start here: What's the point of a patented solution if competitors can find an obvious solution?

When you move into the Non-obvious Zone, you'll add a dimension your competitors lack. They'll be working with project portfolios in the Obvious Zone, balancing Me-Too and Long-Shot projects, blind to non-obvious needs. They'll be squandering resources in the zone of lowest possible R&D efficiency. Meanwhile, you'll be competing where your competitors are not… by asking better questions. You'll be running a race by yourself. Now that's a race you can win.

Endnotes

1. Several experts have concluded companies waste 50-75% of their product de-
    velopment investment: Clayton Christensen (*The Innovator's Solution*, p. 73)
    concluded, "Three-quarters of the money spent in product development invest-
    ments results in products that do not succeed commercially." The authors of the
    APQC Benchmarking Study (*Improving New Product Development Performance
    and Practices*, p. 6) reported, "… only one in four development projects is a com-
    mercial success."

Chapter 9

Principle 5: Develop Your People... Transform Your Business

Problem One and Problem Two
Three Levels of Development
Three Means of Development
Using KAI for Effective Team Problem-Solving
Measuring Your Progress
New Product Development Diagnostic

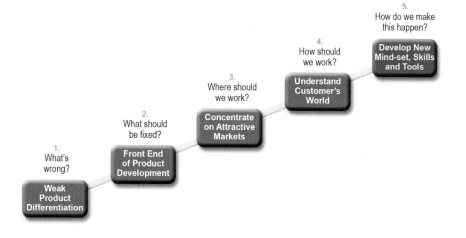

Many business leaders understand that new products are the *lifeblood* of their organization. They know ongoing new product success lets them win greater market share, reap higher prices, increase growth and earnings, advance their careers and enjoy their jobs more. And yet relatively few are able to build their businesses into new product powerhouses. Why is this? I believe they have not solved Problem One and Problem Two.

Problem One and Problem Two

Problem One is knowing *what* must change. It is, after all, a complicated matter. A study by the American Productivity and Quality Center found 77 practices strongly correlate to new product success. Seventy-seven! They concluded, "Product innovation is perhaps the most complex of all business activities, and getting it right is equally complex."[1] And faced with the Tyranny of the Urgent, many leaders simply do not invest the time to sort this all out and develop strong convictions about what simply *must* change.

But even when they solve Problem One, leaders must face the thornier Problem Two—knowing *how* to effect change throughout their organization. Just think what little help they get. Most business books are "What Should Happen" books or "What They Did" books. Even if a leadership team comes to complete agreement around its conference room table on What Should Happen, it faces an enormous gulf before employees are *doing* What Should Happen on a day-in-day-out, no-looking-back basis.

Problem Two is tough because we are talking about changing behaviors. Most of us have a hard time changing our own behaviors, let alone the behaviors of others. For example, coronary bypass surgery provides immediate relief, but seldom prevents recurrences or prolongs life unless the patient adopts a healthier lifestyle. So if your choice was "change or die," what would you do? Unless you are the exception, you would die. Two years after these procedures, 90% of patients fail to change their lifestyles.[2]

> If your choice was "change or die," what would you do? Unless you are the exception, you would die.

So if nine out of ten people would rather die than change, what chance does a business leader have? Some try to avoid this by hiring external consultants to do the work—e.g., voice-of-the-customer research—for them. Frankly, if you are serious about upgrading your new-product machine, this makes little sense. It would be akin to paying your manufacturing staff to continue producing mediocre products, while also paying a contract manufacturer to produce a few outstanding products. You would pay more than you should, sow potential discord and fail to develop an important competency.

If you want to upgrade your new-product machine, you need to upgrade the capabilities of a critical mass of technical and commercial people. If you find this daunting, that's actually a healthy sign. It is one thing to become convinced that your company needs to do more customer inter-

Figure 9.1

Developing People

3 Levels of Development
- New Mind-set
- New Skills
- New Tools

3 Means of Development
- Training
- Coaching
- Follow-up

views. It is quite another matter to reach the point at which technical-commercial teams are routinely and independently conducting such interviews, impressing customers and advancing exciting new product designs. The executive who adopts a "make it so" approach, but fails to invest in the development of employees, will be disappointed. Fortunately, while this is not easy, it is relatively simple. In our experience, you can practically ensure success if you apply three *levels* of development and three *means* of development (Figure 9.1).

Three Levels of Development

1) New Mind-set. Unless people understand and accept the "why," they care little about the "how." The initial phase of development should be an education in underlying principles, such as the importance of front-end work, the need to move beyond product "tweaks," and the rationale for market segmentation. Research is showing that real change is more likely to take place when the motivation is positive, rather than negative.[3] Better to focus on the impact of winning at new products rather than a "burning-platform" rationale or the dire consequences for failing to act.

An effective way for people to adopt a new mind-set is in a safe, intimate learning setting with peers. They should have the opportunity to hear new concepts, the dedicated time to think about these concepts, the freedom to challenge and debate them, and the incentive to apply them. George Bernard Shaw claimed that most people *think* only two or three times per year... and that he had made an international reputation by thinking once or twice a week. Given the frantic pace of business today, it is wise to create an environment for deeper thinking.

2) New Skills. Dr. Deming used to rail against company executives who were heavy on slogans and banners, but light on training employees in skills such as statistical process control. He knew that sustainable competitive advantage required these hands-on skills. Such is the case for New Product Blueprinting. For successful interviews alone, this means developing improved listening skills to really hear customers' ideas, and learning new probing techniques to understand why those ideas are important to them.

> Effective teams benefit from a diversity of problem-solving styles—not just diversity of experience.

Applying problem-solving diversity is another skill to be learned. Highly effective teams benefit from a *diversity of problem-solving styles*—not just the diversity of experience that comes from multi-functional teams.[4] Consider using a powerful tool called Kirton Adaption-Innovation (KAI) to build team awareness and performance in this area.[5] (See inset on following pages.)

3) New Tools. In much the same way one learns to use a new software program, teams must learn to use new tools, such as customer interviewing with a laptop and digital projector, internet-based secondary market research, or digitally capturing the results of a customer site tour. Like any new tool, it is important to learn and then begin using the tool, especially under the watchful eye of an experienced craftsman. This timing is critical. If a team won't be able to immediately begin practicing with a new tool, consider delaying the training until they are ready. Otherwise, they'll forget much of what they learned and will be ineffective.

Three Means of Development

1) Training. Have you ever "read the book" on a subject and then later—perhaps at a seminar or by working alongside someone—realized you had missed some major points? To pass along a new mind-set, skills and tools, especially in a complex subject, often requires a workshop or seminar format. When you do this, allow ample time for team members to learn new material and then engage in role-playing and other exercises to immediately put that material to use. Two additional components for success are the enthusiastic participation of the business leader and real-life projects that teams can work on during and after this training.

2) Coaching. It helps to develop at least one internal expert within your business who can serve as a coach to the teams. This is a "safe" person they can call or invite to team meetings for help at any time. The internal coach often accompanies teams on their initial customer interviews and sits in on critical team decision-making meetings. Some of this coaching may come initially from external experts, but ultimately, you want to own this process. Your well-trained and experienced internal coaches help you do this.

3) Follow-up. In the dismal research on heart surgery patients mentioned earlier, there was a ray of hope. One particular program had a 77% success rate, compared to the average of 10%.[6] A key element of this program was *ongoing support*. No matter how dynamic your initial training or adept your internal coach, follow-up review sessions (often web-conferences) are needed. These sessions can help in three ways.

First, teams can learn important lessons from each others' experiences, so have several teams review their progress at each session. Second, the research suggests that most workshop material will be forgotten unless reviews such as these take place.[7] Third, the crush of daily schedules requires the discipline and accountability of such follow-up. Otherwise workshop participants will return to a mountain of e-mails and brushfires, and—despite best intentions—never quite put their new skills into practice.

Using KAI for Effective Team Problem-Solving

Research and experience have long established that multi-functional teams are more effective than mono-functional teams. Why so? A team containing technical, marketing, sales, production or other functions is a team with *diversity of knowledge*. The diversity comes from different experiences in education, work content and so forth, and allows the team to solve more complex problems. But each of us is more than a bundle of knowledge. Our success in any endeavor is determined by our knowledge, aptitude, drive and problem-solving style.

We certainly don't want a diversity of aptitude or drive: We'd just like bright and motivated teammates. But what about diversity of problem-solving styles? This is where Kirton Adaption-Innovation Theory helps. It posits that we each have a natural, preferred style of problem-solving that lies somewhere on a normally distributed continuum ranging from highly adaptive to highly innovative (Figure 9.2).

Those with a more adaptive style tend to solve problems within existing structure that has been consensually agreed upon by others. Those with a more innovative style prefer to solve problems using less structure. (If you and your spouse are taking a drive, the more adaptive might see a speed limit sign, while the more innovative sees

Figure 9.2

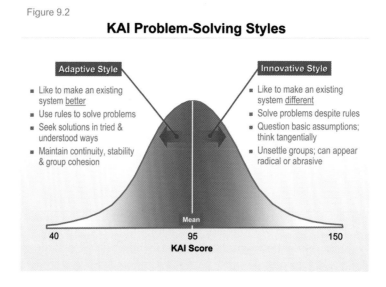

KAI Problem-Solving Styles

a speed *suggestion* sign.) More adaptive thinkers like to make things *better* and are good at implementation and follow-through. More innovative thinkers like to make things *different* and are good at bringing fresh perspective.

Each style works well for some problems… and poorly for others. A highly adaptive team member might have trouble getting "out-of-the-box" when framing a project, while a highly innovative member might get distracted from finishing the project! As shown in Figure 9.3, new product development is actually a series of problems that require both styles. Highly effective teams bring the right problem-solving style to bear precisely when it is needed.

Figure 9.3

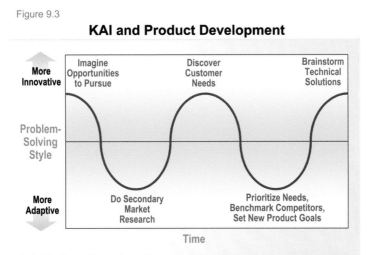

KAI and Product Development

Both Adaptive and Innovative styles are needed for effective new product development.

We use the KAI psychometric inventory with all workshop participants… but this is not about selecting the "right" KAI profiles for the teams. It is about moving team members from *intolerance* to *tolerance* and then to *appreciation*. Without proper understanding, we each tend to think highly of people who think as we do… and wonder what's wrong with those who don't. As teams grasp the power of diversity in problem-solving styles, they not only tolerate those who think differently, they actively seek their input when it's needed. An adaptive thinker in a team full of innovative thinkers might have felt like an outsider before. Now, he might be the hero when it is time to do some thorough market research or write a tight business case.

Measuring Your Progress

Suppose you pursue the three levels and means of development. How do you know if your company is getting better? You could—and should—measure your new product success in the marketplace and your financial reports. But in addition to such *result* metrics, you should also consider *process* metrics. The latter have the advantages of 1) providing feedback much earlier and 2) revealing specific areas where more attention is needed.

Consider how you could benchmark your organization to understand its strengths and weaknesses *and* provide a means to measure improvement. You might find the New Product Development Diagnostic shown in the following pages helpful; there is no charge if you choose to participate. Each participant within a business provides a confidential assessment of how she thinks her business is doing in each of 16 success factors. The results for the entire business are tabulated and they provide a baseline for monitoring improvement. When a business gets serious about measuring its progress year after year in areas that really matter, it builds important strengths over competitors.

Before moving on to Part III, let's review. In Part I, you learned that this book is for B2B companies and profit-minded "builders" within those companies, and you got an overview of the New Product Blueprinting process. In Part II, you explored five principles: 1) Avoid new product incrementalism, 2) work on the front end of your new-product machine, 3) concentrate on market segments that are winnable and worth winning, 4) turn customer interviews into a competitive edge, and 5) transform your business by developing your people.

You may have read quite enough at this point... but if you are forging on, prepare for a mental down-shift. We're going to move from the thoughtful forum of principles to the gritty streets of practice. Part III should provide you with the detail needed to understand New Product Blueprinting at a more concrete, hands-on level.

If you decide to read Part III, a word of warning is in order: At first glance, the seven Blueprinting steps might appear overwhelming. But please bear in mind that most practitioners have learned these steps in four or five days of training spread over several months of practice. When absorbed in a measured manner, the steps are not at all intimidating. I have worked across an extremely broad range of B2B industries and have yet to meet a single business that was unable to implement this process.

Endnotes

1. Paige Leavitt, ed., *Improving New Product Development Performance and Practices* (Houston: APQC International Benchmarking Clearinghouse, 2003), 70.
2. Alan Deutschman, "Change or Die," Fast Company, 94 May 2005, 53.
3. Ibid.
4. Peter K. Hammerschmidt, "The Kirton Adaption Innovation Inventory and Group Problem Solving Success Rates," Journal of Creative Behavior 30 (First Quarter, 1996): 61-73.
5. The Kirton Adaption Innovation (KAI) inventory measures how a person solves problems and interacts with others. For more information on KAI, visit www.kaicentre.com.
6. Alan Deutschman, "Change or Die," Fast Company, 94 May 2005, 53.
7. In 1885 the German philosopher, Hermann Ebbinghaus, conducted a memory study with himself as the subject. His experiment—which has been reproduced often since then, showed that he remembered less than 40% of the items he had memorized after nine hours; beyond this, the rate of forgetting leveled off with time.

New Product Development Diagnostic

Advanced Industrial Marketing (AIM) has been measuring B2B companies' proficiencies in 16 success factors for years. Typical results are shown in Figure 9.4. The ratings are provided confidentially by employees of the company and tabulated by AIM. (This service is provided at no charge at www.newproductblueprinting.com/diagnostic.)

Figure 9.4

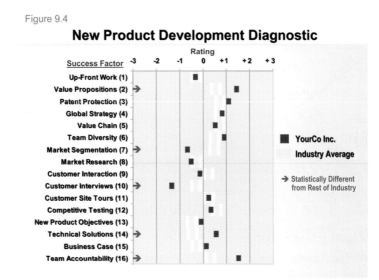

This analysis helps companies address areas of weakness and measure their progress going forward. It may be *interesting* to see how you stack up against the industry average, but that is really not what this is all about. It is about whether you are getting better—moving your ratings to the right—on an ongoing basis.

The following pages briefly describe the relevance of each success factor. In most cases, these success factors are established "best practices," and we can point to research supporting the fact. In other cases, they are "leading practices," and the research is not yet complete. In all cases, experience and reason support these as highly desirable front-end practices for B2B suppliers.

For each success factor, you will also see the definitions for the -3 and +3 ratings that respondents use when they complete the diagnostic.

1. Up-Front Work

Relevance: Up-front homework—when done well—more than doubles the success rate and market share penetration of new products.[1]

-3 Rating: We do little work before the development stage... typically spending < 5% of our total project costs here.

+3 Rating: Over 25% of our project spending is used for pre-development work, e.g., understanding market needs.

2. Value Propositions

Relevance: Well-differentiated products that deliver unique customer benefits provide four times as much profitability as "me-toos." [2]

-3 Rating: All our new products are "me-too" or offer incremental new customer value; we don't get premium pricing.

+3 Rating: All our new products offer superior, differentiated value and command premium pricing as a result.

3. Patent Protection

Relevance: Superior products capture > four times the market share of others[3]... but must be protected via patents or trade secrets.

-3 Rating: None of our new products are protected by patents, and trade secrets provide little or no protection.

+3 Rating: All of our new products are protected by at least one patent, and many by two patents.

4. Global Strategy

Relevance: Chinese imports into the U.S. double every four years, making *reactive* B2B suppliers highly vulnerable.[4]

-3 Rating: We react as needed to competitive products from low-cost global producers and have no global strategy.

+3 Rating: We produce globally, have global market strategies and are aligned with customers who do the same.

5. Value Chain

Relevance: While identifying *end-user's* needs is critical,[5] *immediate* customers are often unable or unwilling to provide this info.

-3 Rating: We interact only with our direct customers and don't understand the impact of our products downstream.

+3 Rating: We interact with our customers' customers and know how our products add value through the value chain.

6. Team Diversity

Relevance: There is a high correlation (0.55) between success & teams' cross-functionality. Diversity of problem-solving styles also helps.[6]

-3 Rating: Our commercial people relay customer needs to our technical people who then do the development work.

+3 Rating: Projects are driven by cross-functional teams using diverse thinking styles to solve complex problems.

7. Market Segmentation

Relevance: Attacking attractive segments is a proven strategy[7]... yet resources are often wasted on pursuing unattractive segments.

-3 Rating: We don't understand our market segments well, and are organized by internal factors instead of markets.

+3 Rating: We have carefully explored market segments and have concentrated resources on the most attractive.

8. Market Research

Relevance: There's a high success correlation (>0.5) for high-quality market information,[8] yet many companies lack modern research tools.

-3 Rating: We occasionally purchase multi-client market research reports on well-established market segments.

+3 Rating: We use internet-based research to probe unique segments, followed by industry expert consultations.

9. Customer Interaction

Relevance: Although customer research drives success,[9] only 11% of companies systematically base their product designs on this.

-3 Rating: Our customer meetings are ad-hoc, and product development is a *reaction* to customers' stated needs.

+3 Rating: We proactively interview customers in targeted segments to uncover unspoken and unimagined needs.

10. Customer Interviews

Relevance: B2B customers (vs. end-consumers) make ideal interviewees... savvy, interested, fewer in # and often known & friendly.[10]

-3 Rating: Our interviews are conducted by commercial people untrained in listening, probing & interviewing skills.

+3 Rating: Highly-trained technical-commercial teams probe, understand and prioritize customers' unmet needs.

11. Customer Site Tours

Relevance: Observation is a great research tool,[11] but few companies use powerful site tour methods to their competitive advantage.

-3 Rating: Customer tours occur only when customers offer them; we seldom gain useful information from them.

+3 Rating: We *pursue* tours, prepare observation checklists and capture & document valuable data from each tour.

12. Competitive Testing

Relevance: Best-practice companies rate highly in this area.[12] When done well, this testing engages customers & boosts pricing.

-3 Rating: Our new products are usually developed without a thorough understanding of competitive products.

+3 Rating: Product development begins only *after* competitive testing based on customer-recommended procedures.

13. New Product Objectives

Relevance: Sharp, fact-based definition *before* development more than triples success rate and nearly doubles market penetration.[13]

-3 Rating: Objectives are internally generated or are a reaction to customer requests. They tend to drift over the project life.

+3 Rating: Our designs are defined sharply and early based on hard, "outside-in" data from customers and competitive testing.

14. Technical Solutions

Relevance: High-quality work drives success (correlation > 0.6).[14] Today this requires engaging the best internal *and* external minds.

-3 Rating: We tend to rely on familiar, internal technologies to achieve our new product objectives.

+3 Rating: We consider novel external technologies and explore a wide range of solutions through brainstorming.

15. Business Case

Relevance: High-quality business assessment correlates with success (0.65)[15]... but many teams are ill-trained to build their case.

-3 Rating: We often begin product development without an approved business case to justify needed resources.

+3 Rating: Our teams build pre-development business cases with the rigor of venture capital investors.

16. Team Accountability

Relevance: Accountable teams are successful (correlation = 0.58).[16] Systems *and* culture drive accountability at the best companies.

-3 Rating: We seldom sound the alarm or take corrective action when projects fall behind schedule or miss targets.

+3 Rating: Teams are held accountable through visible project tracking and regularly scheduled review sessions.

Endnotes for New Product Development Diagnostic

1. Robert G. Cooper and Elko J. Kleinschmidt, *New Products: The Key Factors in Success*. American Marketing Association, Chicago, 1990.
2. Robert G. Cooper, *Winning at New Products, 3rd Edition* (Reading, Mass: Perseus Books, 2001), 83-84.
3. Ibid., 59-60.
4. U.S. Census Bureau.
5. Paige Leavitt, ed., *Improving New Product Development Performance and Practices* (Houston: APQC International Benchmarking Clearinghouse, 2003), 55.
6. Ibid., 46. In addition to this research supporting the value of diversity of experience (cross-functional teams), Dr. Michael Kirton has established the importance of diversity in problem-solving styles: Michael J. Kirton, *Adaption-Innovation: In the Context of Diversity and Change* (London: Routledge, 2003), 202-228.
7. Robert G. Cooper, *Winning at New Products, 3rd Edition* (Reading, Mass: Perseus Books, 2001), 59, 101.
8. Paige Leavitt, ed., *Improving New Product Development Performance and Practices* (Houston: APQC International Benchmarking Clearinghouse, 2003), 45.
9. Robert G. Cooper, *Winning at New Products, 3rd Edition* (Reading, Mass: Perseus Books, 2001), 59.
10. For a full discussion of the advantages associated with interviewing B2B customers over end-consumers, refer to Chapters 1 and 10.
11. D. Leonard and J. F. Rayport, "Spark Innovation Through Empathic Design," Harvard Business Review (Nov-Dec., 1997).
12. Paige Leavitt, ed., *Improving New Product Development Performance and Practices* (Houston: APQC International Benchmarking Clearinghouse, 2003), 56.
13. Robert G. Cooper, *Winning at New Products, 3rd Edition* (Reading, Mass: Perseus Books, 2001), 61
14. Paige Leavitt, ed., *Improving New Product Development Performance and Practices* (Houston: APQC International Benchmarking Clearinghouse, 2003), 45.
15. Ibid.
16. Ibid., 46.

Chapter | **Part I: Overview**

1. This Book Is for B2B... Not Consumer Goods
2. This Book Is for Builders... Not Decorators
3. This Book Is for Maximizing Profits
4. What Is New Product Blueprinting?

Part II: Five Principles

5. Principle 1: Avoid Incrementalism and Its Death Spiral
6. Principle 2: Upgrade Your New-Product Machine
7. Principle 3: Pick Your Battleground Markets Wisely
8. Principle 4: Use Customer Interviews for a Competitive Edge
9. Principle 5: Develop Your People... Transform Your Business

Part III: Seven Steps

10. Step 1: Market Research
11. Step 2: Discovery Interviews
12. Step 3: Preference Interviews
13. Step 4: Side-by-Side Testing
14. Step 5: Product Objectives
15. Step 6: Technical Brainstorming
16. Step 7: Business Case

Part III

Part III reveals the inner workings of New Product Blueprinting. You'll see detailed descriptions, examples and screen shots of Excel® spreadsheets, so you won't have to guess at how things are done.

Chapter 10

Step 1: Market Research

Three Business Types
Three Research Objectives
Market Research Flow Chart
What Information Is Needed?
What Secondary Research Tools Are Used?
Selecting Your Target Segment
Setting Your Project Scope

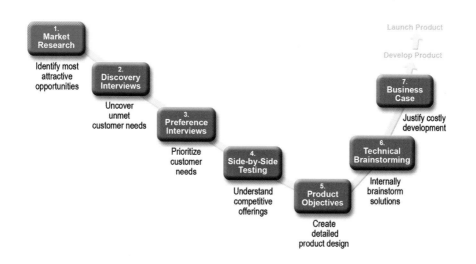

The first step in New Product Blueprinting is Market Research for one simple reason: It makes no sense to develop great products for markets that won't properly reward you. You want to aim your limited resources at a segment that is large, growing, ripe for change and is not filled with suppliers fighting like a pack of hungry dogs over a dry bone.

It may be that you already have an intimate understanding of the segment you are targeting… in which case you could skip Step 1. But if you are pursuing a true market segment—a cluster of customers with similar needs—you still may have more to learn. You may need market research to even *identify* the clusters that exist, let alone determine which are attractive.

Figure 10.1

Market Research Tools

So Many... but Which to Use... and When?

Focus Groups
Customer Interviews by Consultant
Phone Surveys
Observation
Internet Research
Customer Panel
Industry Expert Consultations
Design for Six Sigma
Customer Interviews by Supplier
Conjoint Analysis
Multi-Client Market Studies
Company-Sponsored Market Studies
Quality Function Deployment
Mail Surveys

So where do you start? As shown in Figure 10.1, there are many market research tools to consider. As it turns out, all these tools are appropriate in some situations... but inappropriate in most. To select the best market research tools, it helps to think about the type of business you are in and the characteristics that define it.

Three Business Types

Consider three types of businesses (Figure 10.2), which can be defined by the products they deliver to their markets: 1) *Industrial*, in which components or ingredients are sold to other companies, 2) *Commercial*, in which finished or whole products are sold to other companies, and 3) *Consumer*, in which finished products are sold to consumers.

The first two are B2B and very much the focus of this book. Industrial products are often important to another company's *products*, and Commercial products are often important to another company's *process*. With minor exceptions, the same Blueprinting methodologies are used for both Industrial and Commercial applications.

Figure 10.2

Three Types of Businesses
A Framework for Selecting Market Research Tools

	Industrial B2B Products	Commercial B2B Products	Consumer B2C Products
	Components Sold to Companies (e.g., Specialty Polymers)	Finished Products Sold to Companies (e.g., Computer Servers)	Finished Products Sold to Consumers (e.g., Toaster Ovens)
Number of Customers	10s to 1000s	1000s to 10,000s	10,000s to Millions
Nature of Relationship	Often Very Close	Often Close for Largest Customers	Non-Personal
Collaboration Potential	Potentially High	Often High for Largest Customers	Very Low
Level of Customization	Often High	Possible for Largest Customers	Low
Inter-Customer Competition	High Within Segment	Minimal	None

There are significant differences, though, between B2B (Industrial and Commercial) and B2C (Consumer). Each of the differences shown in Figure 10.2 doesn't hold in every case, but they are relevant in most. B2B suppliers have fewer customers than B2C producers. Even when B2B customer counts run into the tens of thousands, suppliers often have a few large, important customers. A company selling to many restaurants or home builders, for instance, may give special attention to a few restaurant chains or regional builders.

This focus on fewer customers usually leads to closer relationships between B2B suppliers and their major customers. B2B suppliers have the potential—too often unrealized—to collaborate very closely with their most important customers. And this collaboration can put them in the position to customize their products to meet the needs of larger customers.

B2C producers often gather their customers together for focus groups. In some B2B industries, this would be unthinkable as these B2B customers are in fierce competition with each other and would be unwilling to speak up. As with the other contrasts between B2B and B2C, different methods are needed for uncovering customer needs.

Figure 10.2 was created with physical products in mind, but you can see how each of these five characteristics would apply as well to service offerings. For example, imagine you provide liability insurance to chemical companies. Do you have more in common with a home-insurance agent or a raw material supplier? Sure, your "product" looks more like a home-insurance policy than a drum of resin. But *in terms of uncovering your market's needs*, you should behave more like a raw material supplier. Your market research should take advantage of the fact that you can develop a close, collaborative working relationship with a small number of customers.

Three Research Objectives

In addition to considering your business type, you should also think about the *purpose* of your market research. For the front end of new product development, we find it helpful to pursue three research objectives: 1) Understand segment, 2) discover unmet needs, and 3) prioritize unmet needs. These objectives should be pursued stage-wise in this order. So, considering the differences between B2B and B2C businesses, what are the best tools to use for each stage of B2B market research?

1. Understand Segment. Three tools are particularly useful at this point: published research, industry expert consultations and commissioned consultant studies. Published research, such as multi-client studies, are easily located through the internet. For our purposes, an industry expert is someone who has spent most of his or her career in one field and can offer enormous insight with little or no additional research. Commissioned consultant studies are those that you sponsor. Each of these will be explored in more detail later in this chapter.

2. Discover Unmet Needs. One tool stands head-and-shoulders above the rest—the customer interview. B2B customers are often prepared to work with you... partly because you are prepared to design your product to meet *their* needs. Also, you may already have many close working relationships that you can leverage. In New Product Blueprinting, this stage is accomplished in *Step 2: Discovery Interviews*.

3. Prioritize Unmet Needs. For many of the same reasons, the customer interview is also the preferred tool for prioritizing customer needs. For New Product Blueprinting, this is done in *Step 3: Preference Interviews.* While a Discovery Interview is qualitative and asks, "What else would you like to see?" the Preference Interview is quantitative and asks, "How important is this… and how satisfied are you today?" (In some cases, Preference *Interviews* are supplemented with Preference *Surveys.*)

Market Research Flow Chart

The flow chart in Figure 10.3 is the preferred approach for pursuing B2B market segment opportunities. First, you learn all you can through published research, including multi-client research studies found on the internet. If the segment looks unattractive, drop it and move on to the next. If it still looks promising, find and consult with one or more industry experts to learn more. If the opportunity continues to look attractive, advance to customer interviews. The first two steps are considered "secondary research" and the latter—in which your learning is first-hand—"primary research."

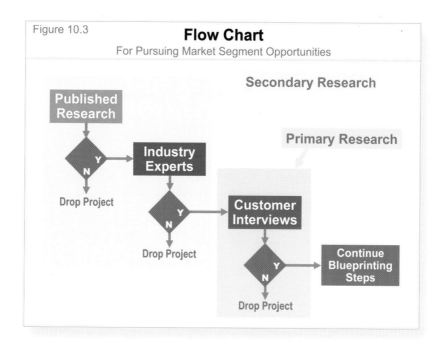

Figure 10.3

Flow Chart
For Pursuing Market Segment Opportunities

This methodology is highly efficient in terms of time spent. Consider the tongue-in-cheek wisdom of the research scientist: "Two months in the lab can save you two days in the library." It is also cost-effective: A new product team might spend $10,000 on market research reports, $100,000 on customer interviews and $1,000,000 on product development. You can save a fortune by learning a project is a dud sooner rather than later. Since we will deal with customer interviews in following chapters, the first research objective—understand segment—will be explored next. Specifically, we will discuss the information needed and the tools used to gather this information.

> A team might spend $10,000 on market research reports, $100,000 on customer interviews and $1,000,000 on product development.

What Information Is Needed?

Many New Product Blueprinting projects start by considering several market segment opportunities simultaneously. The team gathers information on these segments and then selects one to pursue. When several opportunities are considered in parallel instead of in sequence, you improve your odds of pursuing the most attractive. Also, your team will be more willing to drop an unattractive opportunity if they have a runner-up to select. To do this, teams should collect information on ten points. (See "Market Research Shopping List" inset on next page for descriptions.)

1) Market Size
2) Market Structure
3) Market Trends
4) Market Growth
5) Supplier Profitability
6) Unmet Customer Needs
7) Likely Value Proposition
8) Likely Technical Fit
9) Current Market Presence
10) Other Information

Market Research Shopping List

1. Market Size. What is the market potential for a product you might develop? Precision isn't needed now... just the approximate sales ceiling, because this typically differs a *lot* from segment to segment.

2. Market Structure. Who supplies what to whom? Who has the most power in the channel? Where is your best point of entry? You can create a simple value chain diagram to help you determine who to interview later.

3. Market Trends. Consider globalization, government regulation, consumer tastes, substitute technology, etc. You will probe more deeply during interviews, but this can influence which market segment you target.

4. Market Growth. What are the growth prospects for this segment, and why? As a rising tide lifts all boats, so you'll have an easier time in a rapidly expanding market segment vs. a stagnant or shrinking one.

5. Supplier Profitability. How intense is the rivalry within this industry? You don't need precise profit margins, but you want to know if this is one of those industries in which no one makes money. Also try to understand the level of competitive entrenchment and reaction you might encounter.

6. Unmet Customer Needs. Does this market segment have obvious unmet needs? Can you differentiate between those segments that seem satisfied with the status quo and those that seem hungry for change?

7. Likely Value Proposition. Do you have a compelling idea for offering value to this segment? You certainly don't *need* a pre-existing concept, but if you have one, it could be a tie-breaker against other segments.

8. Likely Technical Fit. Is this a good fit with your technical capabilities? Since you haven't probed customers' outcome space yet with interviews, it is premature to dwell on your solution space. Still, it helps to consider if some segments would have a greater likely technical fit than others.

9. Current Market Presence. Are there divisions within your company that currently sell to customers in this segment? When you pursue an existing segment, it is easier to schedule interviews, but you won't gain as much new information as when interviewing completely new segments.

10. Other Information. Is there anything else you should consider when deciding which market segment to pursue? Perhaps your company has made a commitment to grow in targeted areas, has liability concerns about some types of businesses, etc.

Until you begin interviewing customers, your data for some of these criteria—unmet customer needs, for example—may be quite thin. That's OK. Just gather as much secondary market research as possible to improve your odds of selecting the best target segment to pursue.

What Secondary Research Tools Are Used?

As mentioned earlier, three research tools are typically used to understand B2B market segments: published research, industry expert consultations, and commissioned consultant studies.

1. Published Research. There are several excellent internet sites you can use to search for published market research. The following is certainly not a complete list, but provides a good starting point. Please note that these services tend to change frequently, and that the following is current only as of this writing.[1]

www.google.com As Google and other search engines have become more powerful, you can often access published research directly— without searching through the holdings of information brokers. If you are researching the semi-gloss paint market, for example, enter Google search terms such as *semi-gloss market research*, *semi-gloss market size*, and *semi-gloss market growth*. This strategy often helps you find both market research reports available for purchase and individual pieces of data—some of which are free. Particularly in the latter case, try to confirm your data using more than one source.

www.marketresearch.com This service contains more than 100,000 market research reports available from over 500 publishers and consulting firms. If you don't have access to a corporate account for one of the services listed below, this may be your first choice; MarketResearch.com allows you to purchase research with a credit card (corporate accounts are also available). Even if you don't purchase reports from this source, consider registering. This allows you to view report abstracts—which often provide valuable insights.

www.profound.com Recently acquired by MarketResearch.com, Profound offers more than 250,000 research reports from over 170 global research publishers. Unlike MarketResearch.com, you need to have a corporate account to use this service. It contains powerful search functions and can be cost-effective: For many of the larger research reports, you can view the table of contents and purchase only those sections of interest to you. So instead of purchasing a $3,000 report, you might purchase a data table for $30 or a report section for $300.

www.frost.com Comprehensive market research reports (conducted by Frost and Sullivan) can be accessed by browsing a list of market sectors and sub-sectors, or by a text search. Reports may be purchased by credit card or through a corporate account.

www.freedonia.com This service publishes over 100 new research reports annually (conducted by The Freedonia Group), which are available for purchase via credit card. For larger reports, you can preview tables of content and purchase sections of interest.

www.ingentaconnect.com This allows you to search over 30,000 industry publications for more than 20,000,000 articles, chapters and reports. Abstracts may be viewed for free and articles purchased for a fee.

www.onesource.com With this service, multiple users within your company gain unlimited information access for a set annual fee. OneSource provides information on industries, but its greatest strength is in-depth company profiles for over 17 million global companies and 21 million executive profiles.

www.dnb.com This Dun and Bradstreet service has extensive listings of companies by industry classification. You can use this to create marketing lists of prospects or research key prospects or competitors. This is also a good source of hard-to-find information on privately held companies.

2. Industry Expert Consultations. If you are exploring an unfamiliar market segment, consider engaging an industry expert. In many cases, these will be recently retired individuals who have spent all or most of their careers in the industry of interest. They can answer many of your questions without further digging, so in a short time you'll gain valuable insights. And their knowledge extends beyond the dry data you will find in market research reports: A good industry expert won't just recite the players in an industry; she'll know who is winning, who is losing, and who has lost their way. And when you find that expert, she may also help you set up your customer interviews. If she is well-known and respected, she might open doors that would be closed to your team. Here are some ways to find such experts.

www.intota.com This B2B database contains over 10,000 peer-recommended experts in more than 30,000 areas of science, engineering, healthcare, regulation and business. You enter a term for your subject of interest and can then view multi-page resumes of the experts; if one looks like a good match, you can hire this expert for a one-hour consultation or longer. (This service is also available on a subscription basis through Intota's parent company, Guideline.) If you don't find an expert using their web-based search engine, you can engage Intota analysts to search for industry experts not currently listed in their database.

www.amazon.com Perhaps the industry expert you need is a published author: You may be surprised to see how many highly focused and technical topics are covered in the books and e-documents here. Amazon's search engine makes it easy to find books on your subject; then use their SearchInside!™ [2] and "About the Author" features to locate an author of interest to you.

www.eworkmarkets.com This service is used by over 90% of Fortune 500 companies to find experts and consultants. While this is usually done for the purpose of conducting internal company assignments and projects, you may be able to use their database to find an appropriate industry expert.

3. Commissioned Consultant Studies. You may have noticed that the flow chart for pursuing market segment opportunities (Figure 10.3) did not include commissioned consultant studies. This is often a tool of last resort since it can be expensive and time-consuming (by the time you set the project scope, execute the contract, familiarize the consultant and manage to milestones). Also, if you turn over too much of the research to someone else, your team will miss valuable first-hand learning.

There are times when hiring a market research consultant makes a good deal of sense, though. Perhaps you are seriously resource-constrained; you might use a consultant to screen multiple market segments so you can focus on the most attractive. Hired consultants allow you to discreetly scout out a new market without disclosing your interest. They also generally do a good job of providing you with an objective, unbiased perspective.

Consider two types of consulting firms: 1) those specializing in the industry you are targeting, and 2) firms with well-honed secondary and primary research capabilities. The advantage of the first type is that you won't be paying them while they are learning; they already possess a deep understanding of your target market. (In some ways, these firms are a higher-priced version of the industry expert discussed earlier.) You may want to use the second type—skilled generalists—when the first is unavailable or when you have multiple segments to lightly screen.

> www.galegroup.com To find the first type of consulting firm above, contact trade associations for leads. You can access the *Encyclopedia of Associations* at this web-site or by visiting your local library.

> www.greenbook.org Use this service to find the second type of consulting firm. The Green Book provides a listing of firms by type of service offered: Check out their *Business-to-Business* category.

> www.pdma.org The Product Development and Management Association's website has a yellow-page section that lists research firms. These generally have strong skills in market research for new product development projects.

Selecting Your Target Segment

For this and the remaining chapters in this book, imagine you work for Breakthrough Polymers, a company that produces polymers used in paints and other coatings (a fictitious example). Your multi-functional team needs to select its target market segment and set the scope of its project.

You have gathered data on nine possible market segments to pursue: factory-applied wood floor coatings, on-site wood floor coatings, kitchen cabinet coatings, and others. To select one, the team gathers around a projector displaying the Excel screen-shot in Figure 10.4. (All Excel screen-shots in this book are identified by a blue border.) Teams typically begin by considering the seven criteria shown here: *Size, Growth, Profitability, Needs, Value, Technical Fit* and *Market Presence*. Your team first decides if these are the best criteria and makes any needed adjustments.

	SIZE of Revenue Opportunity	Market Segment GROWTH	PROFITABILITY of Segment Suppliers	Unmet Customer NEEDS	Likelihood of VALUE Proposition	Likelihood of TECHNICAL Fit	Existing MARKET Presence
Assign an "A" rating if:	Available market > $50 mil	Growing > 6% per year	Supplier gross margins > 40%	Trends are driving a need for change	We have a novel high-value idea	Protectable solution is fairly likely	We have a strong market presence
Assign a "B" rating if:	Available market in between	Growing between 2% and 6%	Supplier gross margins in between	Customers are open to change	We have some good concepts	We have a good technology fit	We are familiar with this market
Assign a "C" rating if:	Available market < $20 mil	Growing <2% per year	Supplier gross margins < 25%	Customers seem content today	We have no concepts currently	We don't have a technology fit	This market is new to us
Factory-applied wood floor coatings	A	A	A	A	C	C	B
On-site wood floor coatings	A	B	A	C	B	C	C
Kitchen cabinet coatings	B	B	B	B	C	B	B
Interior flat wall paint	A	C	C	C	C	C	C
Semi-gloss paint	A	B	A	A	A	A	A
Exterior gloss paint	B	B	A	A	B	B	C
Coatings for metal parts	C	C	C	B	C	B	B
Wood stains	C	B	B	C	C	C	C
Exterior house paint	A	B	B	B	C	C	C

Figure 10.4 **Screen market segments and select one to pursue with interviews.**

Your team then decides what constitutes an A, B or C for each of the criteria. In the case of *Size*, an A here means the market potential is greater than $50 million, C is less than $20 million and B is in between. Using the market research data gathered earlier, your team enters an A, B or C into each cell, which change color automatically for easy analysis.

Next, your team selects one of these market segment opportunities (rows) to pursue for a potential new product project. Generally, "the more green, the better"… but this can be an over-simplification. Some criteria might be more important than others: For instance, you might not pursue a segment if it doesn't meet a minimum *Size* hurdle. Or perhaps you have new breakthrough technology and your "project" is to determine if and where it might have a good fit. In that case, you'd select market segments to explore for which your *Likelihood of Value Proposition* and *Technical Fit* are strong.

So should you create numerical weightings for each criterion, with an algorithm that scores each market segment? I wouldn't. First, most teams do not have enough real market information for this level of rigor… until they get out there and start interviewing. Keep in mind that your job is simply to select a promising market segment to explore through interviews. Don't get too attached to it: You might drop it after your first interview and move on to another.

Second, be skeptical of algorithms that give you "the answer." (This segment is an 82, so pick it over the one that is 77.) It is better to have a team huddle around a projector with the chart above, engaging in a healthy debate about the best segment to target.

Setting Your Project Scope

In this case, imagine your team selected semi-gloss paint as its target market segment… lots of green and no major drawbacks at this point. You are almost done with Step 1. You'll record your team members, project timeline and, importantly, your *project scope*. This is the phrase that your customers—paint producers—should see displayed on the screen when you are interviewing them.

A good scope might be "production and sale of semi-gloss paint." During Discovery Interviews, you want your customers to talk about *anything that is important to them*… but only within this scope. So if one of them starts describing problems with their clear varnish, you'll say, "OK, I think I understand. Now, coming back to the production and sale of semi-gloss paint…"

Getting the scope right is not always easy. Keep these tips in mind: First, consider both the *who* and the *what*—the target business and the job the business is trying to do. If your target business is the wheat farmer, the job might be clear. But if your target business is construction equipment, you might need to focus on either paving, demolition, earth-moving, hauling or forestry.

Second, your scope might change depending on which business you are targeting within your *value chain*. Suppose you make bearings that are used in a part assembly for trucks. Should your scope encompass the assembly or the entire truck? Consider who "calls the shots" in your value chain and the likely extent of your product's influence... but when in doubt, target the downstream business.

Finally, getting the *breadth* of the scope right is often a bit of a balancing act. Frame it too broadly and you could miss distinct market segment requirements; you'll end up creating an "averaged" product that truly satisfies no one. Frame it too narrowly and the segment might not be large enough to pursue. Do you target hardwood floor coatings? Just gym floor coatings... which might have different impact-resistance needs than bowling alleys? Only college gym floors... which might have different scuff resistance needs than elementary school gym floors? Just do your best job and be prepared to re-frame your scope after a few interviews as you learn more.

You are finished with Step 1. If you have picked a great market segment to pursue, your team might never come back to Step 1 for this project. But we find that many teams have some "outside-in" surprises when they start interviewing. No problem; they just come back to Step 1, update their knowledge and pick the next best segment.

The other time this step is revisited is when others in your company want to benefit from your market research. Many companies keep these project files on central servers. In some cases, scores of business teams within a single company have captured vital New Product Blueprinting market research data in this way. This is an excellent approach to preserve that corporate memory.

Endnotes

1. Perhaps this should go without saying, but all of the services mentioned in this book have been included without any form of consideration or compensation made to the author or Advanced Industrial Marketing, Inc. (AIM). The only criteria for including a service is the expected value that the service *might* provide the reader. It is the responsibility of the reader to exercise due diligence before engaging any of these services.
2. SearchInside! is a trademark of Amazon.

Chapter 11

Step 2: Discovery Interviews

Interview Logistics
Customer Tours
Listening Skills (PEAR Method)
Probing Skills
Customer Outcomes
Discovery Interview Structure
Debriefing after Interviews

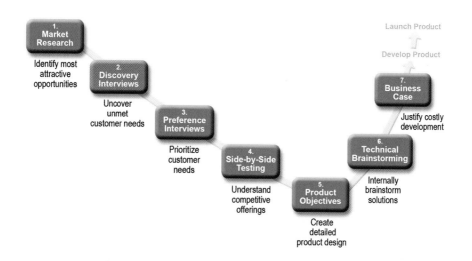

The New Product Blueprinting process calls for two types of interviews: Discovery followed by Preference. During Discovery Interviews, you cast your trawling net broadly to collect as many customer outcomes as possible. During Preference Interviews (next chapter) you learn which outcomes are important to customers and currently not being satisfied. These are the only outcomes customers will reward you for delivering. Give them anything else and they'll just ask you to lower your price.

We are often asked the question, "Do we really need to do *both* types of interviews?" Imagine your semi-gloss paint team decides to conduct only Discovery Interviews. Your team leader has the preconceived notion that customers want better mildew resistance, but customers haven't mentioned this in any Discovery Interview so far. Finally, in your last Discovery Interview the customer—when pressed—says, "Yeah, I guess we could use a little more mildew resistance." Afterwards, your team leader says, "See! I've been telling you all along that customers wanted better mildew resistance!" If you do not use Preference Interviews to convert customer input into hard, unbiased data, your team could easily lose its way.

What if we skipped Discovery Interviews and just did Preference Interviews? Years ago, we used to do this. We would select our favorite ten outcomes and then interview customers to capture their importance and satisfaction ratings for each. But we had two problems with this approach. First, because we had not probed earlier to uncover customers' unmet needs, our ten outcomes omitted the really exciting ones that could have separated us from competitors. Second, we came across as somewhat arrogant. Who were *we* to decide which ten outcomes were most important? Evidently not someone interested in engaging customers.

If you conduct Discovery Interviews, expect your customers to be pleasantly surprised; many say the interview was unlike anything they had experienced before. To pull this off requires new methods and skills on your part. In this chapter we will cover these in seven sections:

1) interview logistics
2) customer tours
3) listening skills
4) probing skills
5) customer outcomes
6) interview structure
7) debriefing after interviews

Interview Logistics

We will address ten fundamental questions here regarding interview logistics. This overview should help you see how an effective Discovery Interview comes together.

1. Who should conduct the interviews? Plan on sending a two- or three-person team to each Discovery Interview. Typically, you will have at least one commercial and one technical person. The technical person is critical: This tells your customer it isn't just another sales call, and that you are serious about capturing customers' input for your new product design. And when both the technical and commercial functions hear the same customer perspective first-hand, it builds effectiveness in your multi-functional team.

2. What are the interviewing roles? You will need a Moderator, Note-taker and (optional) Observer. The Moderator takes the lead, asks most of the probing questions, handles transitions and keeps the interview on topic and on time. The Note-taker records notes on his laptop while they are being projected on a screen or wall. For most of the interview, it looks like he is typing in colored sticky notes that resemble 3M Post-It Notes®.[1] The Observer listens between the lines, forms an overall impression of customer input, and—with the Note-taker—picks up any probing opportunities missed by the Moderator.

3. How do we set up the interview? When you call to set up an interview, you have two objectives. The first is getting the appointment. It helps to write a script ahead of time that includes the points shown in Figure 11.1. Stress

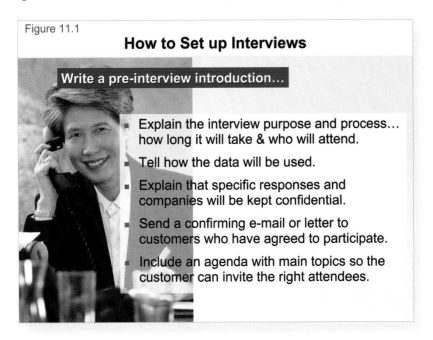

Figure 11.1

How to Set up Interviews

Write a pre-interview introduction...

- Explain the interview purpose and process... how long it will take & who will attend.
- Tell how the data will be used.
- Explain that specific responses and companies will be kept confidential.
- Send a confirming e-mail or letter to customers who have agreed to participate.
- Include an agenda with main topics so the customer can invite the right attendees.

that your company would like to develop a new product, is interviewing several industry experts and would like their input before proceeding. The second objective is getting the right participants: When they agree to the interview, ask who will attend—by name—and review your range of topics so they will invite many different functions (production, technical, marketing, etc.). You could send a world-class interviewing team, but your interview will be a dud if only their summer intern shows up.

4. Do we interview individuals or groups? The advantage of interviewing one person at a time is that the voices of timid or lower-level workers won't get drowned out. But group interviews have the advantage of allowing several individuals to "springboard" off each others' ideas and have more time to think of new ideas. We generally shoot for group interviews, unless we believe the highest ranking person in the room will silence subordinates.

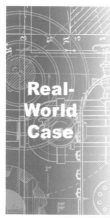

Real-World Case

We were conducting a customer interview with a large group ranging from the business VP to lab technician. For three hours they all debated the needs of their business, discussing what their customers expected, their production capabilities, etc. As we packed up to leave, the VP said, "Hey, I don't have a copy of this. E-mail it to me as soon as you get home!" I realized our competitors would have loved to have been a fly on the wall for that meeting... but we had *facilitated* it.

5. How many companies should we interview? Typically, suppliers interview 6-10 customers in the Discovery step, but more might be required if their secondary research has large gaps or they have a long value chain to explore. A good test is whether or not you are hearing new ideas with each interview. When you start to hear mostly "echoes," it's a good time to stop.

6. Who should we interview? Since your goal is to capture as many outcomes as possible, you will need to expose yourself to a broad range of companies and job functions within those companies. For our semi-gloss paint example, you would interview existing customers, prospective customers and former customers. You'd also move down the value chain and interview some paint contractors. Within each company, you would invite a range of job functions. These could include manufacturing, R&D, marketing, sales, and management. We recommend tracking not only the interviewed companies, but job functions as well to be sure you are exposing your interview team to the broadest range of ideas.

7. Where should we conduct the interviews? Many solid Discovery Interviews have been done at neutral sites such as trade shows, but most are conducted at the customer's facility. This way, you often get a better mix of attendees and may get a facility tour. Get to their conference room early to set up so you can focus on introductions and a brisk meeting kickoff. Consider a room set-up similar to that shown in Figure 11.2… but don't wrestle the customers for the right seat! This set-up is helpful, not essential.

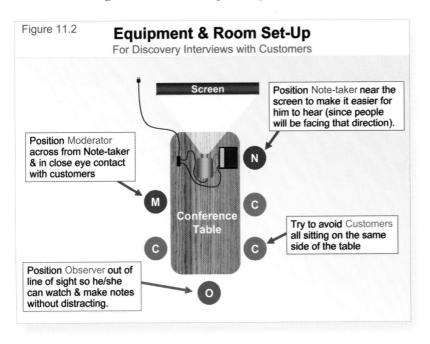

Figure 11.2

Equipment & Room Set-Up
For Discovery Interviews with Customers

Screen

Position Note-taker **near the screen to make it easier for him to hear (since people will be facing that direction).**

Position Moderator **across from Note-taker & in close eye contact with customers**

Conference Table

Try to avoid Customers **all sitting on the same side of the table**

Position Observer **out of line of sight so he/she can watch & make notes without distracting.**

If you have one to three interviewees and no wall or screen for projecting—a construction site for instance—you can use a laptop by itself. Consider using a wireless keyboard so the Note-taker does not block customers' views of the laptop screen.

8. Should we interview under secrecy agreement? It's OK to sign a non-disclosure agreement (NDA) for Discovery Interviews, but is not in your best interest if you can avoid it: You're going to completely stay out of your solution space, right? So you have no confidential information to protect. On the other hand, signing an NDA delays scheduling the interview. If the customer asks for an NDA, you can discourage this by telling them you don't intend to discuss solutions... just *their desired outcomes*. Mention that it's completely up to them what they choose to discuss. Only occasionally will you have to choose between signing and foregoing the interview.

9. Will Discovery Interviews work in any country? Discovery Interviews have been done with great success in every region of the world, but cultural sensitivity is advised. According to the work of Professor Geert Hofstede, Western European and North American companies often exhibit a more egalitarian and individualistic culture than much of the rest of the world.[2] When interviewing companies within a more hierarchal and collective culture, you should consider smaller groups, emphasize the "no wrong answer" rule of idea generation, invite groups at the same peer level and perhaps use a preliminary meeting (vs. a phone call) to set up the interview.

10. What pitfalls should we avoid? Selling and solving. Your commercial people are trained to sell and your technical people are trained to solve... but both groups should simply *search* during the Discovery Interview. Resist the temptation to begin your interview with a presentation on your company's capabilities. And make sure your technical people know they are expected to ask great questions, not share how much they know.

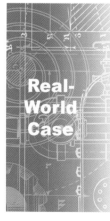

Real-World Case

When the Moderator asked her first question of the customer, her own technical colleague answered it. That was strange, she thought, but went on to a second question. The same thing happened. This went on for several minutes as her body language escalated from stern glances to a kick under the table... which finally worked. As she later told her colleague, "If I wanted to hear what *you* had to say, we could have done this back at our office and saved the airfare!"

A related pitfall is to bias the interview by telegraphing a solution you already have. If you own exciting technology you think might be useful, keep it to yourself. Then, if the customer independently volunteers outcomes that are a good fit with your solution, you'll know you're on the right track. Otherwise, change solutions or market segments.

Customer Tours

Whenever possible, arrange for a tour of your customer's facility, and schedule this to occur just prior to the actual interview. Explain that this will give you a frame of reference for understanding their needs during the interview. The customer tour is typically conducted with just one of your customer contacts, so it won't consume too much total customer time.

The key to a successful tour is preparation. As shown in Figure 11.3, there are many areas to explore. We recommend you preassign the type of information each team member looks for during the tour. Then just before the tour, ask your customer contact to help you draft a quick sketch of the process that you can carry with you. You can use this during the tour to orient yourself and to scribble notes and questions for the Discovery Interview.

Figure 11.3

Customer Tour Checklist

What possible outcomes can you observe?

Capacity Increases	• The customer's production line or cells could run faster • There could be less production downtime • Changeover time could be reduced between product runs
Improved Quality	• The customer's product could have fewer defects • Scrap, waste or recycle could be reduced • Final product could be more uniform in key specifications
Reduced Material Costs	• Another raw material or part could be eliminated • A less expensive co-raw material or part could be used • Our product could be used for all customer product types • Our product could be more concentrated or functional
Reduced Labor Costs	• A production step could be completely eliminated • Two production steps could be combined • Off-line prep of parts or materials could be simplified • Preparation of parts or materials could be done cheaper
Other Benefits	• Packaging materials could be reduced • Less energy could be consumed • The customer's product could be improved in any way

During the tour, keep a sharp eye out for "work-arounds"—not-so-elegant fixes used to address rate-limiting steps, bottlenecks, frustrations and other problems. After a while, customers become blind to these, and you can bring a fresh perspective. You can learn a great deal by watching workers perform tasks, observing posted production records, looking at the rework area and—when it's safe and you have permission—asking operators questions about what they are doing.

I asked my client if they had learned anything new on their Discovery Interviews. They looked a little shell-shocked as they recounted their last customer tour: "We learned that our customer had found an entirely new way of applying our product that we had never even heard of. The product we *had* been going to develop would have been totally worthless!"

Listening Skills

Don't expect a good interview if your team is not listening well. Overlooking this blinding flash of the obvious has damaged more than a few interviews. Have you ever found yourself rehearsing what you will say next instead of listening intently? Or turning everything the speaker says into a story that relates to *your* experiences? Or assuming you know what the speaker is about to say? Or placating with "right... sure... know what you mean," while only half-listening?

These and other roadblocks limit what you learn from the speaker... and what the speaker is willing to tell you. Such habits can be so ingrained that our coaches have learned to correct them immediately during workshop role-playing. Otherwise the listener often doesn't realize he or she is even doing it.

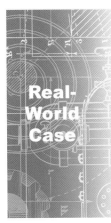

He was a technical wizard and extremely enthusiastic about beginning Discovery Interviews. Only problem was he seemed hardwired to answer all of his own questions: "So, Mr. Customer, can you tell me about this part of your operation? For instance, I know it can take a long time to..." He wasn't giving customers enough credit to think on their own and was too concerned he might appear ignorant. With coaching, he eventually learned that silence often precedes some real gems from the customer.

There aren't any cheap tricks to make you a better listener. There are some helpful habits and reminders, but good listening starts with good attitudes. How well do you do against the checklist in Figure 11.4? It takes hard work and practice to get into this frame of mind, but it is powerful indeed.

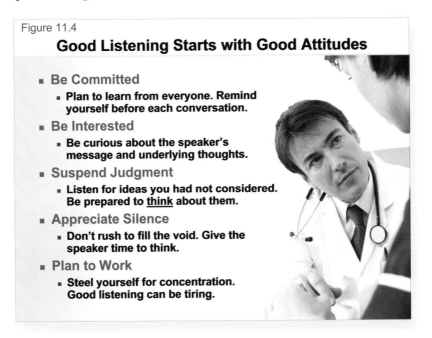

Figure 11.4

Good Listening Starts with Good Attitudes

- **Be Committed**
  - **Plan to learn from everyone. Remind yourself before each conversation.**
- **Be Interested**
  - **Be curious about the speaker's message and underlying thoughts.**
- **Suspend Judgment**
  - **Listen for ideas you had not considered. Be prepared to think about them.**
- **Appreciate Silence**
  - **Don't rush to fill the void. Give the speaker time to think.**
- **Plan to Work**
  - **Steel yourself for concentration. Good listening can be tiring.**

While good attitudes are necessary, they're not sufficient. Give yourself two listening goals: 1) to really listen and 2) to appear like you're really listening. Have you ever seen a speaker disengage because the listener didn't appear to be listening? To avoid this, we have developed the PEAR method for monitoring listeners' *Posture*, *Expression*, *Activity* and *Response*.

You communicate you are listening with your *posture* when you face the speaker directly, lean forward slightly, and keep an open position. Your *expression* communicates interest when you look thoughtful, keep steady eye contact and smile with affirming nods. You say "I'm listening" when your *activity* is minimal... a quiet, still body, with only small gestures. Most powerful of all, your *response* communicates interest when you make affirming comments, recap messages, and ask insightful probing questions.

Probing Skills

The story is told of an old man who believed—as did the ancient Greeks—that the earth was resting on the back of a giant turtle. He was once asked, "Really? Then what is the turtle resting on?" He squinted his eyes, leaned forward and replied, "You're not getting me on *that* one. The turtles go all the way to the bottom!" So we consider "turtling" *getting to the bottom* of what customers want. Imagine the dialogue shown in Figure 11.5, between a Moderator and customer. At first, the Moderator doesn't know where the conversation will lead, but *gradually* begins to understand that she has uncovered an area of great interest to the customer.

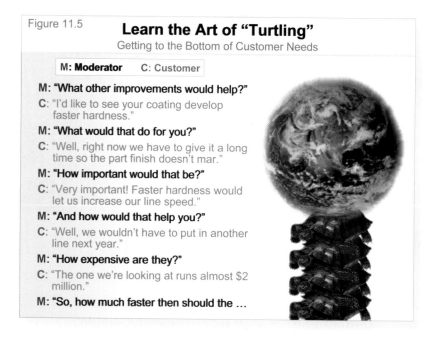

Figure 11.5

Learn the Art of "Turtling"
Getting to the Bottom of Customer Needs

M: Moderator   **C: Customer**

M: "What other improvements would help?"
C: "I'd like to see your coating develop faster hardness."

M: "What would that do for you?"
C: "Well, right now we have to give it a long time so the part finish doesn't mar."

M: "How important would that be?"
C: "Very important! Faster hardness would let us increase our line speed."

M: "And how would that help you?"
C: "Well, we wouldn't have to put in another line next year."

M: "How expensive are they?"
C: "The one we're looking at runs almost $2 million."

M: "So, how much faster then should the ..."

Engaging Speakers with the PEAR Method

One of your goals in an interview is to keep the speakers speaking. You can do this by communicating that you are truly interested in what they are saying… with your posture, expression, activity and response. If you want to get very good at this, review the list below with your team before every interview. Then immediately afterwards, ask your interviewing partners how you did. Of course, they'll say, "Just fine." That's when you say, "No, *really*… I want to hear how I can get better." This gives them permission to help you and reminds them to observe you closely at each interview.

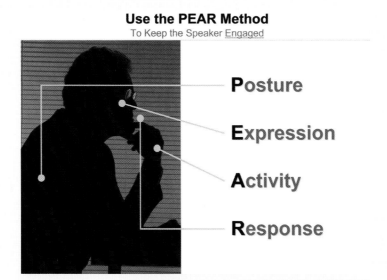

Use the PEAR Method
To Keep the Speaker Engaged

How listeners communicate:	"I'm Listening"	"I'm Not Interested"
Posture	· Face speaker directly · Lean forward slightly · Open (unfolded arms)	· Slouched in chair · Hands behind head · Crossed arms & legs
Expression	· Interested, thoughtful · Good eye contact · Affirming nods, smiling	· Wandering eye contact · Bored expression · Distracted appearance
Activity	· Quiet, still body · Small gestures only · Example: Clasp hands	· Fidgeting · Drumming fingers · Glancing at watch
Response	· Affirming comments · Recapping key points · Great probing questions	· Off-subject comments · "Right…Uh-huh…Sure…" · "That reminds me of… me"

This exchange would not have occurred in a supplier-driven, question-naire-based interview... and this is a critical distinction with Blueprinting interviews. If you interview using the all-too-typical VOC list of 20 questions, you will often miss the good stuff found by turtling. Sure, you feel good filling in those 20 blank spaces, but you learn what's important to you, not your customers. With turtling, you begin a line of questioning and have *absolutely no idea* where the customer will take you. This can be quite exhilarating... but of course, so is running as fast as you can while blind-folded. That's why role-playing is needed to build skills and confidence.

If you are the customer, will you feel more engaged if you are helping a supplier fill in *their* questionnaire... or if the supplier is asking you intelligent, probing questions about matters important to you? Now add one more dynamic: As the customer, your responses will be projected on a screen in sticky notes—in fact lots of sticky notes—which a) treats your ideas with great respect, b) allows you to make corrections, and c) sets an expectation that you will be generating lots of ideas.

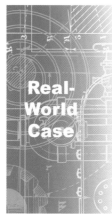

Real-World Case

Two gentlemen at one of our workshops were highly experienced interviewers. They had been interviewing as partners for years, could anticipate each others' moves and were two of the finest traditional-VOC interviewers I had seen. I couldn't wait to hear their first report after trying a Blueprinting Discovery Interview. They described it as "incredible." Not only were they learning more, they were "leading the witness" less. Besides uncovering critical new needs, they squashed ideas they had *assumed* were important... and had already begun working on in their lab!

Here is the final kicker on Blueprinting Discovery Interviews: They are actually much *easier* to do than traditional VOC interviews. Once an interviewing team becomes comfortable with "running blindfolded"—not knowing where the customer will take them—they find their workload goes down.

I have seen traditional VOC teams spend an enormous amount of time developing brilliant questions, getting the sequence just right, tweaking the wording, etc. But regardless of how smart these interviewers are, they are not as smart as their B2B customers—which is why they are interviewing them in the first place. So we use extremely simple questions that require very little preparation and give control to the customer, such as:

1) "What else is important to you?"
2) "Could you give me an example of that?"
3) "How big a problem is that for you?"
4) "Could you help me understand that better?"
5) "Why is that important to you?"
6) "What would happen if you could do that?"

Customer Outcomes

The above probing techniques deliver a wealth of information about customer needs… but we can do even better. We divide everything that comes out of the customer's mouth into three categories: 1) background, 2) solutions and 3) outcomes (Figure 11.6).

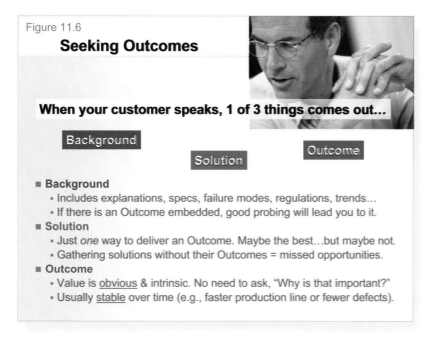

Figure 11.6

Seeking Outcomes

When your customer speaks, 1 of 3 things comes out...

Background   Solution   Outcome

- **Background**
  - Includes explanations, specs, failure modes, regulations, trends...
  - If there is an Outcome embedded, good probing will lead you to it.
- **Solution**
  - Just *one* way to deliver an Outcome. Maybe the best...but maybe not.
  - Gathering solutions without their Outcomes = missed opportunities.
- **Outcome**
  - Value is obvious & intrinsic. No need to ask, "Why is that important?"
  - Usually stable over time (e.g., faster production line or fewer defects).

Background: When you hear the customer provide background information, you don't know if it could lead to an outcome or not. So you probe to see if the current situation is less than ideal. You might ask, "Any problems with this today?" If the customer is less than totally satisfied, then you try to find the outcome that would make him satisfied. Otherwise, move on.

Solution: When you hear the customer offer a solution, you know there is an outcome lurking nearby. Never be satisfied with this solution alone, since it is only *one* way of delivering the outcome—and often not the best. To uncover the underlying outcome, ask, "What would that do for you?"

Outcome: If the customer offers an outcome—or you have probed background or solutions to reach one—your next job is to understand how it is measured. For this, create an "outcome statement"... a sentence with the structure, Verb – Unit of Measure – Object. [3] Example: "Decrease fading of paint exposed to sunlight."

How does this probing technique help? First, the entire point of Discovery Interviews is to uncover as many customer outcomes as possible. Using the above approach is efficient because you are always on an "outcome search," not getting side-tracked with discussions that lead elsewhere. Second, reducing outcomes to explicit outcome statements eliminates misunderstandings. Imagine your semi-gloss paint customer said they wished their paints were "easy to clean." Without further probing, you would not know which of these outcomes (or many others) they actually wanted you to deliver:

A. Decrease physical effort required to remove dirt marks.
B. Increase likelihood that common cleaners will remove dirt marks.
C. Decrease level of visible stains left by common foods.

Wouldn't it be a shame to spend your development time and dollars on a product that did a great job of "A" when your customers were really looking for "B" or "C"? Using the sticky notes in Blueprinting Discovery Interviews, your customers will actually help you create these outcome statements. This minimizes confusion and maximizes engagement.

Discovery Interview Structure

You have just completed a tour of the customer's facility and have regrouped in their conference room for the Discovery Interview. Now what? Start with a three-part introduction: 1) Review the purpose of the meeting, 2) cover the agenda, and 3) explain you are using a projector for one reason: so they can help you get it right. Then launch into the Discovery Interview, which contains the five parts shown in Figure 11.7.

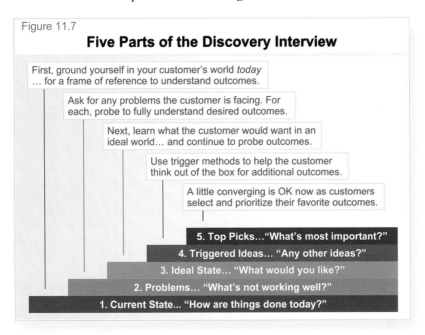

Figure 11.7
Five Parts of the Discovery Interview

First, ground yourself in your customer's world *today* ... for a frame of reference to understand outcomes.

Ask for any problems the customer is facing. For each, probe to fully understand desired outcomes.

Next, learn what the customer would want in an ideal world... and continue to probe outcomes.

Use trigger methods to help the customer think out of the box for additional outcomes.

A little converging is OK now as customers select and prioritize their favorite outcomes.

5. Top Picks..."What's most important?"
4. Triggered Ideas... "Any other ideas?"
3. Ideal State... "What would you like?"
2. Problems... "What's not working well?"
1. Current State... "How are things done today?"

1. Current State. This portion of the interview accomplishes four goals:

- Clarification: Clear up any areas of confusion for you.
- Context: Provide a solid grounding for the interview.
- Completion: Fill in any gaps in secondary market research.
- Comfort: Ease customers into more challenging questions later.

The last point is the most important. You want to put customers at ease so they are fully engaged moving into *Part 2: Problems*. Interviewers who have been trained in traditional VOC methods sometimes make the mistake of dragging the *Current State* portion of the interview out far too long. It should last no more than 15-20 minutes. If it does, customers will feel like you're trying to fill in *your* survey, not ask them about *their* concerns.

2. Problems. Most of us love to talk about our problems; we just can't find anyone to listen for long! When you project a Problems Noteboard (Excel screen shot in Figure 11.8) on a screen, the customers *know* you are interested. Every time they mention a problem, the Note-taker records it in one of the yellow sticky notes. Then the Moderator asks probing questions while the Note-taker types follow-up responses in the *same* sticky note. (The text scrolls so a long string of information can be recorded.)

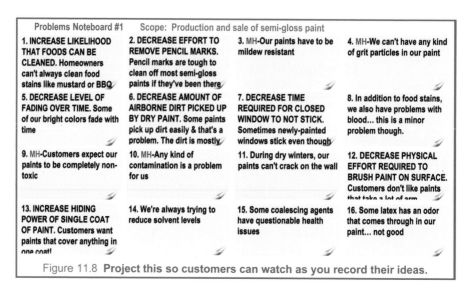

Figure 11.8 **Project this so customers can watch as you record their ideas.**

When the Moderator has "turtled to the bottom," he might create an outcome statement in all-caps at the top of the note. Then the Moderator asks, "Anything else?" and they move on to the next note for a new problem. If something is a "Must-Have" (something absolutely required), it is marked "MH" so the product design doesn't overlook this critical requirement.

3. Ideal State. When the customer runs out of problems, the Moderator moves on to the third part: *Ideal State.* Instead of telling you what is wrong today, customers tell you what could be right tomorrow… their wish-list. Beyond this—and a different sticky note color—the mechanics of the interview are exactly the same as with Problems.

4. Triggered Ideas. Have you ever been in a brainstorming session that seemed like it was over… only to have a skilled facilitator use "trigger methods" to extract many more ideas from the group? Trigger methods help you break out of old patterns of thinking and can lead to 30% more new ideas. Some of these methods can seem a bit bizarre, though, so we have designed several "customer-safe" trigger methods for use during Discovery Interviews.

One of these is called the "Benefits Map." You tell customers there are only three ways for any company to increase profits: increase sales, increase price or reduce costs.[4] Hand out copies of this map (Figure 11.9) and ask if it triggers any new ideas for their business. Perhaps "S4" reminds them they lost business to a competitor and could regain it if their product was improved in some way. Any ideas generated are then recorded on more sticky notes.

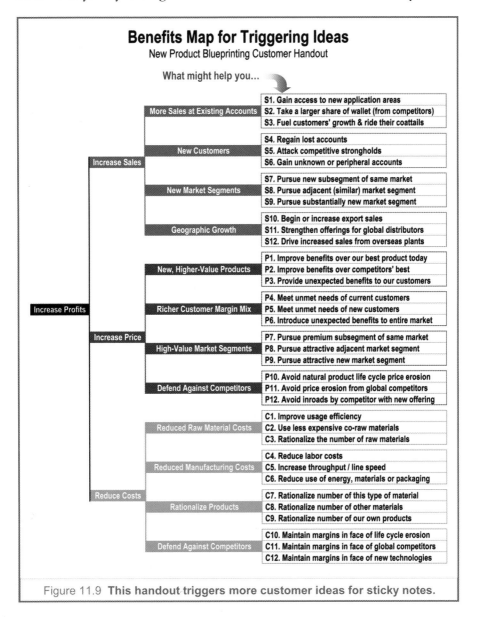

Benefits Map for Triggering Ideas
New Product Blueprinting Customer Handout

What might help you...

	More Sales at Existing Accounts	S1. Gain access to new application areas
		S2. Take a larger share of wallet (from competitors)
		S3. Fuel customers' growth & ride their coattails
Increase Sales	New Customers	S4. Regain lost accounts
		S5. Attack competitive strongholds
		S6. Gain unknown or peripheral accounts
	New Market Segments	S7. Pursue new subsegment of same market
		S8. Pursue adjacent (similar) market segment
		S9. Pursue substantially new market segment
	Geographic Growth	S10. Begin or increase export sales
		S11. Strengthen offerings for global distributors
		S12. Drive increased sales from overseas plants

Increase Profits

	New, Higher-Value Products	P1. Improve benefits over our best product today
		P2. Improve benefits over competitors' best
		P3. Provide unexpected benefits to our customers
Increase Price	Richer Customer Margin Mix	P4. Meet unmet needs of current customers
		P5. Meet unmet needs of new customers
		P6. Introduce unexpected benefits to entire market
	High-Value Market Segments	P7. Pursue premium subsegment of same market
		P8. Pursue attractive adjacent market segment
		P9. Pursue attractive new market segment
	Defend Against Competitors	P10. Avoid natural product life cycle price erosion
		P11. Avoid price erosion from global competitors
		P12. Avoid inroads by competitor with new offering

	Reduced Raw Material Costs	C1. Improve usage efficiency
		C2. Use less expensive co-raw materials
		C3. Rationalize the number of raw materials
Reduce Costs	Reduced Manufacturing Costs	C4. Reduce labor costs
		C5. Increase throughput / line speed
		C6. Reduce use of energy, materials or packaging
	Rationalize Products	C7. Rationalize number of this type of material
		C8. Rationalize number of other materials
		C9. Rationalize number of our own products
	Defend Against Competitors	C10. Maintain margins in face of life cycle erosion
		C11. Maintain margins in face of global competitors
		C12. Maintain margins in face of new technologies

Figure 11.9 **This handout triggers more customer ideas for sticky notes.**

5. Top Picks. Picture dozens of sticky notes containing customer outcomes, all of which can be easily viewed and sorted on the projection screen. The customers have been doing most of the work until now—and enjoying it—so let's keep that going. You ask them for the outcomes they would most like to see improved. These are their *Top Picks*, which you drag to the top of the Discovery Sheet (Figure 11.10). You may wish to code these "TP" so you can easily collect them later.

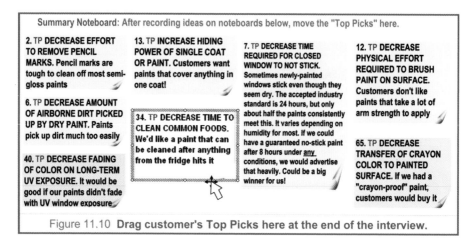

Figure 11.10 **Drag customer's Top Picks here at the end of the interview.**

Most of the Discovery Interview is a divergent thinking process: You are doing all you can to expand the range of possible outcomes to work on later. During the last part—Top Picks—you begin the convergent thinking process. After all your Discovery Interviews are done, you'll use these customer-generated Top Picks to select ten outcomes for your Preference Interviews, which furthers the converging process.

Debriefing after Interviews

Have you ever visited a customer with a colleague, read their call report later and said to yourself, "Well, I *thought* I was on that visit!" This happens due to poor memories, attention lapses, and filtering information according to our own experiences and biases. Since Discovery Interviews provide the foundation for your new product development, you need to make sure this doesn't happen. The best safeguard is to debrief with your team *immediately* following the interview.

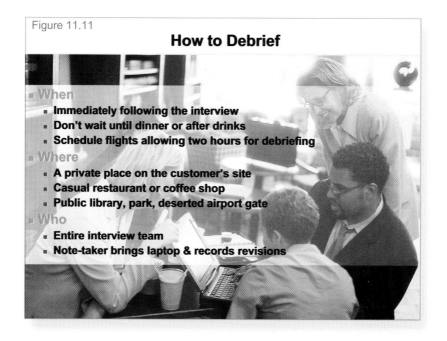

Figure 11.11

How to Debrief

■ **When**
- ■ Immediately following the interview
- ■ Don't wait until dinner or after drinks
- ■ Schedule flights allowing two hours for debriefing

■ **Where**
- ■ A private place on the customer's site
- ■ Casual restaurant or coffee shop
- ■ Public library, park, deserted airport gate

■ **Who**
- ■ Entire interview team
- ■ Note-taker brings laptop & records revisions

In the late 1800s, Ebbinghaus proved something quite frightening about our memories: Unless we recall and review new information within 24 hours, we will forget about half of it.[5] So your interviewing team should allow two hours of time together (perhaps at a nearby coffee shop) to sit around the Note-taker's laptop (Figure 11.11). During this time they accomplish several critical tasks:

1) Edit the Top Picks, clarifying and expanding as needed.
2) Compare and record the key take-aways from the interview.
3) Agree on follow-up actions for this particular customer.
4) Learn how each team member can get better at his or her role.
5) Discuss any needed course corrections for the project.

Discovery Interviews accomplish two things. First, you'll consider customer outcomes in your product design that competitors have missed. Several forces work together to give you a broad collection of clearly-articulated outcomes: the focus on a single market segment, the customer-directed nature of the interview, the clarity of outcome statements and the use of trigger methods. As you converge on your new product design, you will be driven by customers' desired outcomes while your competitors are driven by their hunches and desired solutions.

The second benefit is that the Discovery Interview sets you apart from other suppliers. Customers are used to being "sold to" by their suppliers—not listened to—and this truly gets their attention. But be sure your customers don't have the occasion to say, "Great interview by that supplier… too bad we never heard from them again." As shown in Figure 11.12, there are many ways to keep the engagement going. Make sure you use them!

Figure 11.12

To be avoided at all costs…

"Great interview…
but we never heard from them again."

10 Simple Ways to Build Customer "Engagement"

1. Thank-you e-mail, note or gift
2. Follow-up thank-you call
3. Phone call to clarify some points
4. Schedule Preference Interview
5. Share generalized industry results of your interviews
6. Call or e-mail to indicate project is still active
7. Ask your sales rep to provide them periodic updates
8. Ask customer how he'd like to be updated… and do it
9. Ask customer to review results of side-by-side testing
10. Share new product prototypes with customer

Endnotes

1. Post-It® is a registered trademark of 3M.
2. Geert Hofstede, *Cultural Consequences* (Thousand Oaks, CA: Sage Publications, 2001).
3. Tony Ulwick developed this outcome "dissection," which we find extremely useful for three reasons: 1) When the interviewing team has reduced an outcome to this form, they know their "turtling" is done and they can move on to the next outcome. 2) This form forces the customer to remove ambiguity that could otherwise be included. 3) This structure describes how the outcome is measured and, as such, greatly simplifies *Blueprinting Step 4: Side-by-Side Testing*. See Anthony W. Ulwick, *What Customers Want* (New York: McGraw-Hill, 2005), 29-30.
4. The Benefits Map was built on Jim Hlavacek's work detailing twelve ways to increase operating profit. See James D. Hlavacek, *Profitable Top-Line Growth For Industrial Companies* (The American Book Company, 2002), 266.
5. In 1885, the German philosopher, Hermann Ebbinghaus, conducted a memory study with himself as the subject. His experiment—which has been reproduced often since then, showed he remembered less than 40% of the items he had memorized after nine hours; beyond this, the rate of forgetting leveled off with time.

Chapter 12

Step 3: Preference Interviews

Selecting Outcomes for Preference Interviews
Preference Questions to Ask
Market Satisfaction Gaps
Gathering Preference Data
Modifying Your Market Segment Definition

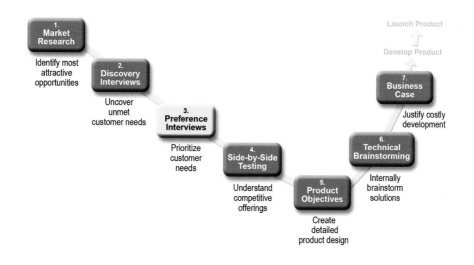

Preference Interviews provide hard data telling you what customers want you to work on. More often than not, this leads to surprises: What customers want and what their suppliers *thought* they wanted are often two very different things. For many suppliers, it's hard to see their lovely theory attacked by a brutal gang of facts. The only thing harder would be to spend the next year and a million dollars developing that theory into a new product... which is *then* attacked by a brutal gang of facts.

Selecting Outcomes for Preference Interviews

As shown in Figure 12.1, most people embark on new product initiatives with a few untested ideas of what they think their new product should do. I

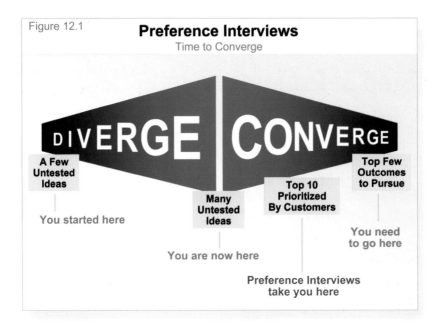

Figure 12.1

Preference Interviews
Time to Converge

DIVERGE | CONVERGE

A Few
Untested
Ideas

You started here

Many
Untested
Ideas

You are now here

Top 10
Prioritized
By Customers

Top Few
Outcomes
to Pursue

You need
to go here

Preference Interviews
take you here

once worked for an excellent Dutch businessman who said we had "romantic notions" of what customers wanted. He was right. Most teams cling to these notions, refusing to challenge, expand or replace them by asking the final authorities—those who vote with their purchasing dollars. You can still test your notions with New Product Blueprinting, but the *quantification* of customer preferences in this step often shows that customers would rather have you work on something else.

After Discovery Interviews are finished, you typically have dozens of Top Pick outcomes; these must be reduced to ten for Preference Interviews. For this, you review all the Discovery Interview sheets and record in one place those outcomes customers named their Top Picks. Then your team sorts, edits and votes on ten outcomes you'll ask about in Preference Interviews.

Why ten? If you were doing consumer goods interviews, it could be many more since a) you are paying them to sit there and answer your questions, and b) you are not taking time to ask about test procedures—since they are not experts. Given the level of detail required for good B2B interviews, experience shows you can generally hold their interest for ten outcomes.

Don't worry that your new product should address 15 or 20 outcomes, and that ten has artificially limited you. Once you see the Market Satisfaction Gaps for your top ten, you will likely want to pick no more than half of them to target for improvement. The others usually score low enough to be of little interest for your new product design.

How can you be sure to pick the *right* ten outcomes for Preference Interviews? Several factors help:

1) The sorting process is done by your entire team, helping to ensure individual bias does not prevail.
2) Customer-driven factors—e.g., the number of times an outcome was cited as a Top Pick—influence the selection.
3) During Preference Interviews, you'll ask customers if you missed an important outcome, so you can revise your set of ten.

Preference Questions to Ask

The crux of the Preference Interview is asking customers five questions about each of your ten selected outcomes:

1) How important is this outcome to you?
2) How satisfied are you with what you can get today in this outcome?
3) What test procedure do you recommend to measure this outcome?
4) What test result would make you totally satisfied?
5) What test result would you consider to be barely acceptable?

There are some additional questions—to cross-check results and learn about preferred suppliers, for instance—but these five are the critical ones. The first two help you generate a Market Satisfaction Gap for each outcome—a quantitative measure of how eager the customer is for you to improve this outcome. The last three help you set up and interpret your side-by-side testing in Blueprinting Step 4. Note the wording in questions 4 and 5: "totally satisfied" and "barely acceptable." You'll see in the next two chapters that this precise wording is used to link customer interviews (Step 3) with side-by-side testing (Step 4), creating an extremely powerful "outside-in" viewpoint that would otherwise be impossible. By linking Blueprinting steps in this manner, the entire process becomes more than the sum of its parts.

When you ask customers the first two questions above, you are looking for ratings between 1 and 10. So that these numbers make sense, you provide definitions to "anchor" the 1-10 scales. For instance, when you ask how *important* it is to "increase the hiding power of paint," you tell them ratings of 5 and 10 mean "moderately important" and "critical," respectively. (Their 1-10 response is called the IMP rating.) When you ask how *satisfied* they are today with their ability to achieve this outcome, ratings of 5 and 10 mean "barely acceptable" and "totally satisfied." (Their 1-10 response here is the SAT rating.) Without such anchors, you wouldn't know how to interpret the resulting Market Satisfaction Gaps.

Market Satisfaction Gaps

Market Satisfaction Gap (MSG) measures market segment eagerness for improvement in an outcome. MSG is nothing more than the product of average market segment *Importance* and *Dissatisfaction* (where the latter

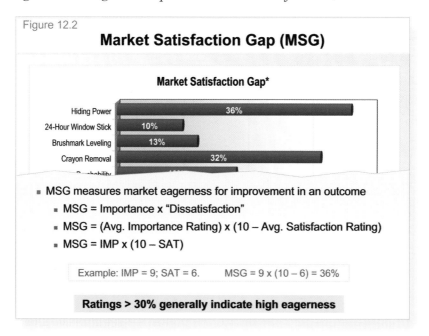

Figure 12.2

Market Satisfaction Gap (MSG)

Market Satisfaction Gap*

Hiding Power	36%
24-Hour Window Stick	10%
Brushmark Leveling	13%
Crayon Removal	32%

- MSG measures market eagerness for improvement in an outcome
  - MSG = Importance x "Dissatisfaction"
  - MSG = (Avg. Importance Rating) x (10 – Avg. Satisfaction Rating)
  - MSG = IMP x (10 – SAT)

Example: IMP = 9; SAT = 6.   MSG = 9 x (10 – 6) = 36%

Ratings > 30% generally indicate high eagerness

Figure 12.3

Market Satisfaction Gaps

If the outcome is very important, a modest level of dissatisfaction is enough for MSG = 30%

equals ten minus *Satisfaction*). So if the outcome "Hiding Power" received an average IMP rating of 9 from customers in your market segment, and an average SAT rating of 6, the MSG would be 36% (Figure 12.2).

Experience shows that outcomes registering around 30% MSG or higher are good targets for improvement. Figure 12.3 displays the combinations of IMP and SAT scores for 30% MSG, as well as for 40% MSG and 50% MSG. An MSG above 50% is rare. The market segment would have to consider a "critical" outcome (IMP of 10) to currently be less than "barely acceptable" (SAT rating < 5), for example. Care should be used in applying the above 30% guideline: In some cases, successful new products have been launched based on attacking multiple outcomes in the 20-30% range.

There is more to interpreting these gaps, but the key point is that they should drive your new product design… or whether the project is even allowed to continue. When your team looks at an MSG profile such as Figure 12.2, they can gain great insight into a market segment's needs. Each profile will tell you a story if you'll spend a little time reading it. Imagine two very different profiles.

What would you do if all ten outcome MSGs were below 20%? Perhaps this is a mature, slowly-changing market segment, and its needs have been largely met over time. You might ask your team, "So, what *other* project shall we work on?" If this market segment is already well-served and satisfied, go after one that is not. Even if your new product delivered on some outcomes, these customers would probably just push you to lower pricing. (You might make an exception if you can apply low-end, disruptive technology to lower customer costs in a way you could protect.[1])

What kind of story would lie behind a Market Satisfaction Gap profile with *many* outcome MSGs above 30%? You would know that the market is currently under-served and dissatisfied. Perhaps the market is relatively new or undergoing rapid change, and suppliers have not yet "caught up." Or consider this more ominous situation faced by a client:

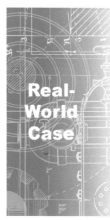

Most of the MSGs were above 30%, and one was above 60%! What was happening? The supplier had been selling expensive production equipment into this market for many decades. But since it was a niche market, it had been a *long* time since a new equipment model had been introduced. As this client wisely noted, "I'm glad we learned how ripe our customers are for change. We're really vulnerable if we don't develop a new product before our competitors figure this out!"

Gathering Preference Data

This data can be gathered both through interviews and surveys. We recommend at least a half-dozen face-to-face interviews be conducted before any surveys, for three reasons. First, interviews are needed to explore test procedures. This requires good probing, which you can't do by sending out surveys. Second, Preference Interviews are a great opportunity to learn more about the customer's world. Imagine that during a single interview one participant gives an outcome a SAT rating of 9, and another participant calls it a 3. Don't average their results: Let them debate their points of view. If you listen and probe well, you will learn a lot about problems in their operations, what their customers are demanding, etc.

Finally, the face-to-face Preference Interview is another good opportunity to engage the customer. Make sure you take advantage of this by interviewing the largest and most important prospects and customers in the segment. These Preference Interviews will resemble Discovery Interviews since laptops and projectors are used and the same interviewing roles apply.

For market segments with many customers, a Preference *Survey* is an excellent way to supplement interviews and build statistical confidence. These surveys are often e-mailed to customers, but you can use other approaches such as phone-, web- and mail-surveys. We also find that holding a web-conference interview can be an effective compromise between face-to-face interviews and surveys: You have the opportunity for good probing without the cost and time commitment of a face-to-face interview. Consider this approach when you already have a solid relationship with the customer.

Modifying Your Market Segment Definition

If you were doing surveys for a consumer goods market segment, you would likely weight each individual's response the same. But this may not be the best way to handle B2B Preference data. Perhaps one of the customers holds 20% of the market share in this segment. You could weight this company's responses at 20%. Or imagine you needed three separate interviews at one company. You could weight each interview at one-third the weight of similar companies. This weighting ability essentially allows you to *define* your market segment.

This capability also allows you to test for market segment integrity. Later in *Step 5: Product Objectives*, you'll be able to see if the customers in your market segment agree with each other or not on outcome Importance and Satisfaction. If not, you may have your arms around more than one market segment. If that is the case, you could assign a 0% weighting to some companies to see if it makes the segment more uniform in its views. If it does, you should look for an explanation and consider excluding these companies from your market segment.

The beauty of Preference Interviews is that they provide you with *facts* for your new-product machine. These facts may tell you to kill the project now. Or they may give you the confidence to pursue it much more aggressively than you otherwise might have.

Endnotes

1. Clayton M. Christensen and Michael E. Raynor, *The Innovator's Solution*, (Boston: Harvard Business School Press, 2003), 45. The authors recommend low-end disruption as an effective means to "attack the least-profitable and most over-served customers at the low end of the original value network."

Chapter 13

Step 4: Side-by-Side Testing

Why Do This Testing?
Customer-Centric Testing
Managing Side-by-Side Test Data

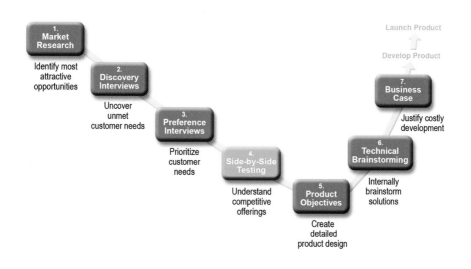

You have gathered one type of outside-in data: customer needs. Now it is time to gather the second: competitor capabilities. You will test customers' best alternatives using procedures they recommended… to determine how well top outcomes can be met by competitors.

If you have any existing off-the-shelf products, you will include these in your testing. Whether you have a current product to test or not, it is important to understand what your competitors' products can do *before* you enter the costly development stage. There are four reasons for this.

What Is Side-by-Side Competitive Testing?

... A rigorous, objective comparison of your best products today
... against the best alternatives available to your customers
... using the test procedures most meaningful to your customers
... for the purpose of designing a product of superior value.

Why Do This Testing?

First, you need side-by-side testing so you can make well-informed product design decisions. Many companies develop products in isolation and are blind-sided by existing competitive products. In other cases, companies forego a wonderful opportunity to understand competitors' weak points... so their own product design can soundly trump them. In either case, it's much too late to gauge competitive positions after you enter the development stage—or worse—the launch stage.

Second, this testing lets you continue engaging large, important customers. Consider two scenes: In one, the supplier's sales rep introduces their new product using a technical sheet based on tests that are obscure or irrelevant to the customer. In the second scene, the customer sees testing *she* recommended and—surprise—the new product performs very well.

Third, many projects go through a "testing stall" during the product's development stage. After new technology is developed, it can take months to then create the test methods to determine if the new technology is "working." It is better to establish these tests before moving into this high-burn-rate stage—even if the tests are simplified for screening purposes.

Fourth, this testing allows you to capture the full value of your new product. To truly "ring the bell" profit-wise, any new product you develop must meet two conditions:

A) Your product delivers an outcome customers highly value.

B) Your customers can't get this outcome elsewhere at a similar cost.

If you only *interview* customers, you will learn about "A" but not "B." To learn about "B" requires competitive testing. You need to look at all your customers' alternatives from *their* perspective and do this in a quantitative manner. Otherwise, you will most likely leave money on the table when you price your new product.

Oddly, the more your product does for customers, the more money you'll probably leave on the table. You usually know where to price an undifferentiated product, because similar products have already established its value. But how do you price a product that does what no product has done before? Imagine you price your new blockbuster at a 20% price premium, without fully understanding the impact of this new-to-the-world product. You might have been able to double the price based on customer value-in-use.

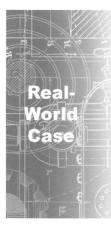

Real-World Case

Our client did a superb job of interviewing down the value chain. When it came to side-by-side testing, they looked at dozens of alternatives. Based on what they learned, they priced their product at a 400% price premium! Eventually, they modified their business model, capturing even more value by producing the entire system that used their novel product.

Customer-Centric Testing

It is not a novel concept to do competitive side-by-side testing. It's done all the time. What is rare is testing that a) is done early in the product development process, b) eliminates supplier-bias and c) truly represents the needs of customers in a targeted market segment. There are four elements to New Product Blueprinting that ensure the latter happens: First, you test outcomes customers care about instead of the ones you care about. Discovery and Preference Interviews guide you directly to these outcomes. Since these are often unexpected outcomes, many suppliers find they need to learn new test methods to properly measure these outcomes.

Second, your testing considers those competitive products deemed most worthy by customers. Specific questioning during Preference Interviews is aimed at uncovering the identity of these products. This often leads to surprises for suppliers, who had previously tested only against obvious and sometimes "easy" benchmarks. You may uncover competing alternatives available to customers that look *nothing* like your traditional competitors, because they are based on entirely different approaches and technologies than your planned new product. These are easy—and painful—to miss.

Third, you use test procedures that are most meaningful to customers. During Preference Interviews, you ask customers how to measure if an outcome is being satisfied... and you rely heavily on this information for your testing. It is important to choose the right test procedures as this leads to better design decisions and builds customer confidence. Also, it avoids the situation in which the customer says, "Wow... you did a *lot* of work! But could you rerun your tests at this temperature instead?" See Figure 13.1 for tips on selecting the best test procedures.

> To be avoided: "Wow... you did a *lot* of work! But could you rerun your tests at this temperature instead?"

Finally, you use the customer's perspective for interpreting test results for each outcome. You gain this perspective during Preference Interviews by asking customers for test results they associate with "barely acceptable" and "totally satisfied." It would be easy to skip this step, but it is critical that you learn "how good is good enough" from the customer's point of view. Otherwise a heavy dose of guessing and supplier bias will enter into your product design decisions. (If you are a "House of Quality" practitioner, you can probably see how this extensive B2B customer interaction lets you eliminate the need for constructing any house matrices at all.)

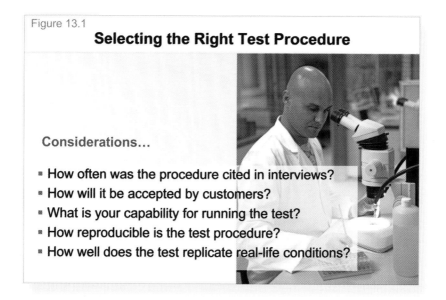

Figure 13.1

Selecting the Right Test Procedure

Considerations...

- How often was the procedure cited in interviews?
- How will it be accepted by customers?
- What is your capability for running the test?
- How reproducible is the test procedure?
- How well does the test replicate real-life conditions?

Sometimes it's a simple matter to set up testing for an outcome. There may be an existing ASTM test procedure, for instance, which will suffice. In other cases, you need to get a little inventive. Perhaps you're considering the outcome "Increase softness of fabric" and there is no "soft-o-meter" available from Acme Test Equipment Co. In this case you might arrange some test samples, with cashmere labeled 10, burlap labeled 1, and several intermediate fabrics labeled in between. You would then have a panel do a blind assessment against these standards, assigning a number to each sample in your side-by-side testing. While it is more work to design your own test procedures, it can be a source of enormous competitive advantage.

Managing Side-by-Side Test Data

You have tested *customers'* most important, unsatisfied outcomes, using test procedures *customers* prefer against competitive products *customers* like best, and interpreted the results using *customers'* perspectives. So far, so good. Now what do you do? You have a great deal of data, but the units of measure, targets and even products tested may be quite dissimilar.

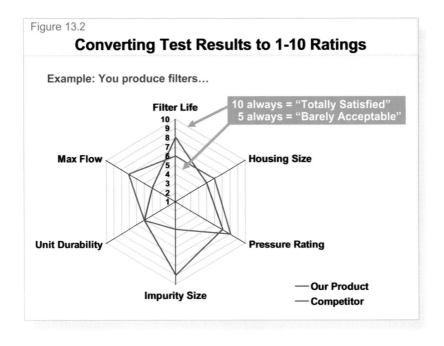

Figure 13.2

In the New Product Blueprinting process, all test results are converted to 1-10 ratings. As you will see more fully (in *Step 5: Product Objectives*), this allows you to compare multiple outcomes and competitive products at the same time. Figure 13.2 offers one example of how the data can be displayed when you do this. Two simple rules are followed: First, a higher rating on a 1-10 scale is always better for the customer than a lower rating. So if the customer is looking for a small filter housing size, you'll assign *higher* 1-10 ratings to *lower* cubic inch volume displacements. This will greatly simplify your work when it's time to visually interpret the data.

Second, the 1-10 ratings are anchored, so 10 means the test result would totally satisfy the customer, and 5 would be barely acceptable. You can do this only because of the way you conducted Preference Interviews. (Specifically, you anchored customers' 5 and 10 SAT responses at "barely acceptable" and "totally satisfied," respectively, and asked for the test results they would associate with "barely acceptable" and "totally satisfied.") Without this anchoring, a chart such as Figure 13.2 *could* be scaled to deliver practically any message the chart-maker wanted. But with the anchoring, any audience can quickly interpret any results for any project in your company.

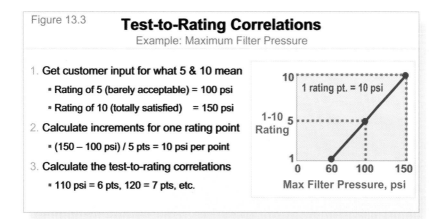

Figure 13.3

Test-to-Rating Correlations

Example: Maximum Filter Pressure

1. Get customer input for what 5 & 10 mean
   - Rating of 5 (barely acceptable) = 100 psi
   - Rating of 10 (totally satisfied)   = 150 psi
2. Calculate increments for one rating point
   - (150 – 100 psi) / 5 pts = 10 psi per point
3. Calculate the test-to-rating correlations
   - 110 psi = 6 pts, 120 = 7 pts, etc.

1 rating pt. = 10 psi

1-10 Rating

Max Filter Pressure, psi

The actual conversion of test results to 1-10 ratings is straightforward. An example is given in Figure 13.3 for the filter unit mentioned earlier. In this case, customers said it would be unacceptable if the filter rating was less than 100 psi. Furthermore, they said the filter would never see a pressure greater than 150 psi… so anything beyond this would be unnecessary. Now you have established your 5 and 10 ratings for specific test results on the outcome "filter pressure."

All that's left is a bit of interpolating and extrapolating so that any test result can be converted to a 1-10 rating (Figure 13.3). If you are using Microsoft Excel to manage your project, it's best to let the software do these calculations so your team can focus on other matters. (Note: Some rare situations call for something other than the linear correlation shown here.)

What about customer specifications? If customers give a specification your new product must meet, you should ask, "And would it help if the product delivered anything *beyond* this specification?" Let's say their specification was "filter must withstand 100 psi." If they answered, "Sure, we'd like an extra safety margin beyond 100 psi," then you have the situation described in Figure 13.3. But if they say, "Nope… all we need is 100 psi," then you have uncovered a "Must-Have"… something both necessary and sufficient. Must-Haves are recorded so you don't miss them later in your product design. But don't waste one of your ten outcome slots on a Must-Have when doing Preference Interviews. You already know the customers' answer: It's very important (IMP = 10) and is now being satisfied (SAT = 10).

When you complete Blueprinting Step 4 in your project, most of the "heavy lifting" is over: The remaining steps tend to take place fairly rapidly. Compared to most companies' projects, your team has amassed far more outside-in information at a far earlier point in time. Now your team will use this to create a new product design (Step 5), develop some preliminary "solution" paths to pursue (Step 6), and justify aggressive development spending through a business case (Step 7).

Chapter 14

Step 5: Product Objectives

Review Interview Data
Review Side-by-Side Test Data
Set Product Design Targets

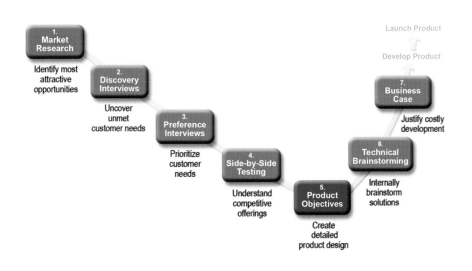

Many teams find this step to be a new and refreshing experience: planning a new product design using crystal-clear, outside-in data instead of personal hunches. You'll lock yourselves in a conference room with a digital projector, and keep the trays of party food coming until your team emerges with its new product design.

As shown in Figure 14.1, this task is greatly aided when you use visual tools that progressively build a story and provide "outside-insight" from multiple vantage points. These visual tools can all be generated within Excel and should be driven by the interview and side-by-side test results entered by the team in earlier steps. Let's return to the example in which your team is designing a new polymer for use in semi-gloss paints.

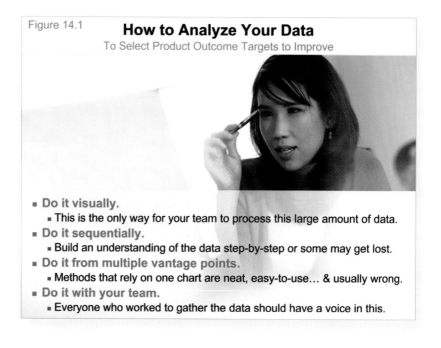

Figure 14.1
How to Analyze Your Data
To Select Product Outcome Targets to Improve

- **Do it visually.**
  - This is the only way for your team to process this large amount of data.
- **Do it sequentially.**
  - Build an understanding of the data step-by-step or some may get lost.
- **Do it from multiple vantage points.**
  - Methods that rely on one chart are neat, easy-to-use… & usually wrong.
- **Do it with your team.**
  - Everyone who worked to gather the data should have a voice in this.

Review Interview Data

Figure 14.2 is displayed on the projection screen. (This and the remaining blue-bordered charts in this chapter were created in Excel.) This chart provides you with 1-10 ratings for IMP (Importance) and SAT (Satisfaction) independently. The results are shown for your entire market segment… as you defined it in *Step 3: Preference Interviews* when you decided which customers to include and how they should be weighted. This chart also displays the standard deviation for each outcome, which tells you how much customers in the market segment agree with each other.

In this case, customers agree that outcomes such as hiding power and brush mark leveling are very important. But look at the wide band for sprayability: Some customers think this is quite important while others do not. Perhaps some paint producers sell to homeowners, who usually apply paint with brushes… while others sell to paint contractors, who spray anything that doesn't move. You can test this hypothesis by isolating the customers in each of these more focused segments and then viewing these charts individually. This could lead you to develop two different products or perhaps design a single product robust enough for both segments.

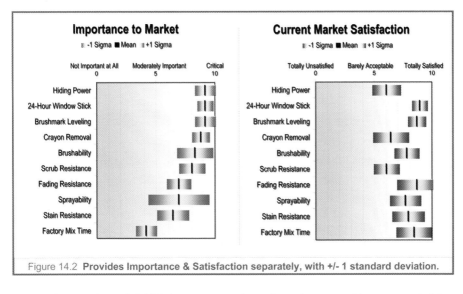

Figure 14.2 **Provides Importance & Satisfaction separately, with +/- 1 standard deviation.**

Next, the IMP and SAT data are combined as shown in Figure 14.3. You would not design your new product around bubbles near the bottom of this chart: Outcomes that are not important to your customers shouldn't be important to you either. You are really looking to improve outcomes in the northwest corner—very important with low current satisfaction. But you don't want to forget those in the northeast corner. These are very important and are *already* being satisfied: Your new product design shouldn't ask customers to do with much less than what they are already getting here.

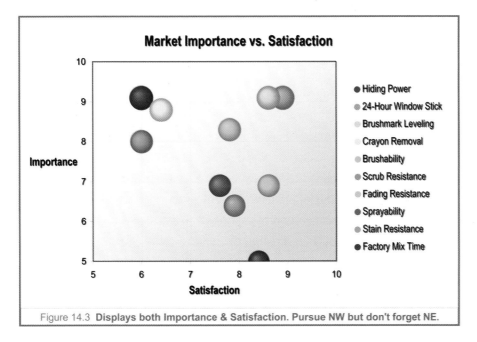

Figure 14.3 **Displays both Importance & Satisfaction. Pursue NW but don't forget NE.**

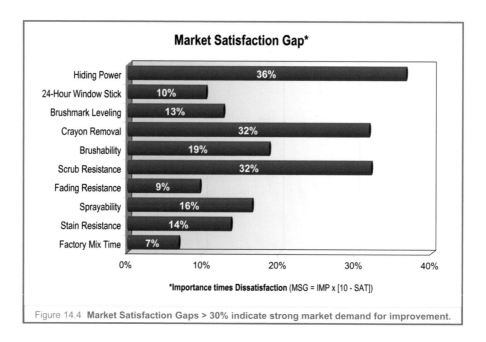

Figure 14.4 **Market Satisfaction Gaps > 30% indicate strong market demand for improvement.**

Figure 14.4 is the most important and frequently used chart, because it efficiently communicates what customers really care about. As described earlier, Market Satisfaction Gap is the product of average Importance and Dissatisfaction, or IMP x (10 – SAT). In general, MSG scores in the teens represent weak demand, scores in the 20s indicate moderate demand, scores in the 30s reveal strong demand and scores in the 40s or higher indicate very strong demand. You are generally on solid ground if you are targeting outcomes above 30% MSG. This information helps you avoid squandering precious resources on outcomes customers don't care about... a very common occurrence within most companies.

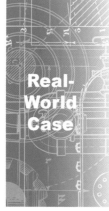

Real-World Case

We were having a web-conference to review a client's Market Satisfaction Gaps. I pointed to one Outcome and said, "For example, you'd *never* want to design your product around this, since it has an MSG of only 7%." I heard a chuckle and the client said, "*Actually*... before Blueprinting, we had planned on making that the main part of our new product design."

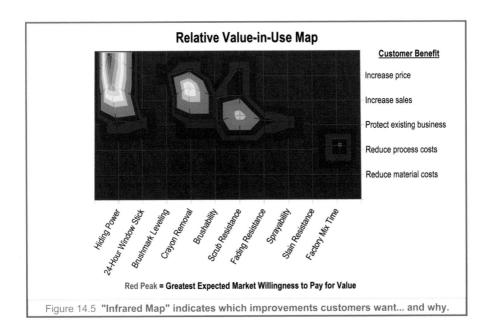

Figure 14.5 **"Infrared Map" indicates which improvements customers want... and why.**

Figure 14.5 provides added insight into *why* customers care about certain outcomes. During Preference Interviews, customers are asked a few extra questions: which of the ten outcomes are their favorites, what benefits they would receive if these outcomes were improved, and how aggressively they would like to see each pursued.

This chart displays the results of these questions. The highest peaks are formed for those outcomes most frequently cited as a favorite and requested for most aggressive pursuit. Figure 14.5 is typically used for three purposes: 1) cross-check Market Satisfaction Gap results, 2) provide insight for new product pricing, and 3) indicate how the product might be best promoted.

Review Side-by-Side Test Data

The previous four charts were created based solely on the results of customer interviews. Figure 14.6 now combines the results of your side-by-side testing with interview data. The "Outside-In Score" predicts how favorably a market segment will view a product. If a product in your side-by-side testing did so well that it totally satisfied customers (SAT = 10) for all ten outcomes, it would have an Outside-In Score of 100%.

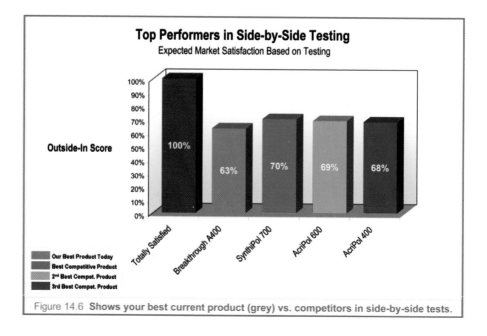

Figure 14.6 **Shows your best current product (grey) vs. competitors in side-by-side tests.**

The Outside-In Score is not a simple average of the ten sets of test results; rather it weights each outcome test according to the importance (IMP) the market assigned to that outcome. So it should accurately represent the market view: Outcome selection, outcome weighting, test procedures and test interpretations are all driven by customers in the target market segment. In the polymer-for-paint example, your team tested several products. This chart displays your company's best product (Breakthrough A400) in the grey column, and the top three competitors in blue, green and violet.

Your team may find the Outside-In Score chart a bit sobering: It's not often we are faced with a totally unbiased view of how our products stack up. The silver lining is that the same can be said for your competitors. But unlike your competitors, you now have a way to conceive various new product designs… and then predict market reaction *before spending a fortune on development.* First, though, you need a bit more information.

Figure 14.6 begs the question, "But why did we score 63% and our best competitor score 70%?" The answer is displayed in Figure 14.7. For each outcome, actual test results have been converted to 1-10 ratings. (Remember, a rating of 5 means barely acceptable to customers and 10 means they are totally satisfied.)

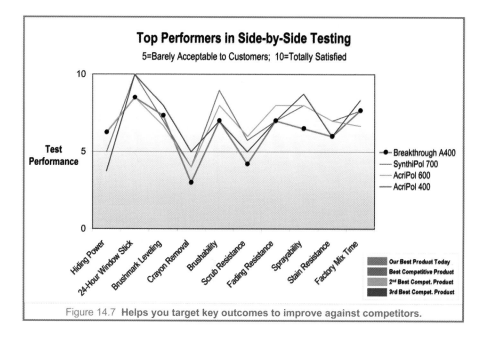

Figure 14.7 Helps you target key outcomes to improve against competitors.

In this example, your team might decide to improve Crayon Removal and Scrub Resistance—since your best current product currently falls below the "barely acceptable" line (rating = 5). For all the charts in *Step 5: Product Objectives*, outcomes are displayed in descending order with the most important on the left. Since Hiding Power is the most important outcome to customers, your team might also try to put some "daylight" between you and your competitors for this outcome.

Before settling on target outcomes, you would review the other charts again. In Figure 14.4, all three of these outcomes—Crayon Removal, Scrub Resistance and Hiding Power—have Market Satisfaction Gaps above 30%. And the same three outcomes all show good peaks in Figure 14.5. Based on this, your team decides these are indeed suitable areas to pursue. But how *much* should each outcome be improved?

Set Product Design Targets

Your team sets its preliminary targets for the above three outcomes based on how the new product would perform using the test procedures you es-

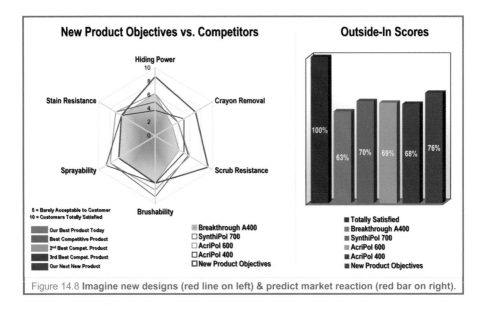

Figure 14.8 **Imagine new designs (red line on left) & predict market reaction (red bar on right).**

tablished in *Step 4: Side-by-Side Testing*. Figure 14.8 gives your team a visual display for creating some "what-if" new product designs in the left radar chart. (Note the number of outcomes has been reduced from ten to six, for display purposes only in this chart.)

Your existing product is shown in grey and top three competitors in blue, green and violet. Your new product design is displayed as a red line. Since the red line rests on the gray border for Brushability, Sprayability, and Stain Resistance, you can see there is no planned improvement for these outcomes. But improvement is planned for Hiding Power, Crayon Resistance and especially Scrub Resistance. If your new product could achieve these red-line test results, it would generate the Outside-In Score shown in the red column in the right chart.

It may be that your team will develop and launch a new product according to this design… and then move on to other opportunities. On the other hand, your new product might be the first in a series of new products… especially if some require longer-term R&D before they are "ready for prime time." In this case, consider creating a Future Product Roadmap, as shown in Figure 14.9. Will your team create multi-generational products that look *exactly* like this? Not likely. But having such targets gives clear direction to your technology development efforts.

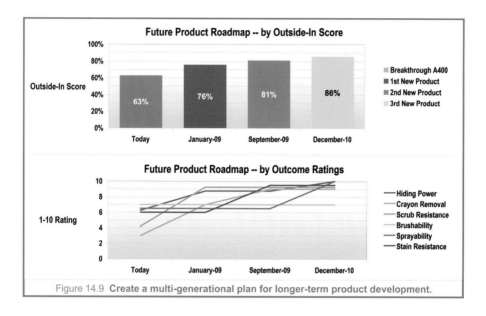

Figure 14.9 **Create a multi-generational plan for longer-term product development.**

Imagine what can happen when your R&D or engineering department has a clear direction of what would most excite customers in the *future* products they develop. This is a powerful "guiding force" for them as they perform their own experiments or review external technologies that might be in-licensed.

It's one thing for your team to wish for these product designs, but quite another matter to achieve them. Great product design creates tension between your aspirations—what you *want* to do—and your abilities—what you *can* do. The latter is addressed in *Step 6: Technical Brainstorming*. You should prepare yourself for some iterations between the worlds of "want" and "can." Think of it as the place where outcomes meet solutions.

Chapter 15

Step 6: Technical Brainstorming

Technology Development vs. Product Development
Open Innovation
Step 1: Set up Meeting
Step 2: Generate & Record Ideas
Step 3: Break Old Thinking Patterns
Step 4: Prioritize Ideas

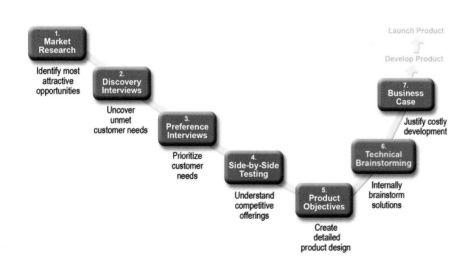

Now it's time to move from "outcome space" to "solution space." This can be cathartic for those who normally lead with their solutions and have been biting their tongues through Steps 1-5. Strangely though, some teams fail to attack this step as aggressively as they should, perhaps because they don't already have the technology in their back pocket. Our advice: You have diligently explored outcomes; be just as diligent in exploring solutions.

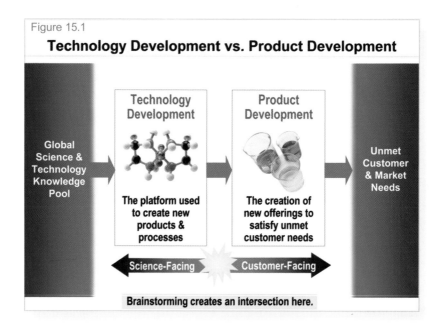

Figure 15.1

Technology Development vs. Product Development

Technology Development vs. Product Development

One of the most effective ways to generate solutions is through brainstorming. While most business methods have short runs of popularity, brainstorming has enjoyed widespread use since Alex Osborn introduced it in the 1940s. In New Product Blueprinting, we use it in a specialized manner: to create an intersection between "solution space" and "outcome space," and specifically *between technology development and product development.*

Technology development converts money into knowledge, while product development converts knowledge back into money.

As shown in Figure 15.1, technology development is "science-facing" while product development is "customer-facing." Many companies fail to differentiate between the two, creating serious difficulties. Technology breakthroughs are "scheduled" to meet artificial deadlines, and product launches are delayed when technology challenges outstrip internal capabilities.

The two processes are quite different: Technology development converts money into knowledge, while product development converts knowledge back into money. Happily, you need not limit yourself to knowledg ated *by your company*. You can use others' knowledge and pay them ba their investment when *you* are ready to use it.

Exposing yourself to the broadest possible range of relevant knowledge is the key. As noted by Segway inventor Dean Kamen, "Invention is the art of concealing your sources." Seriously, doesn't a great deal of innovation occur when someone leaves their familiar Old World to explore a New World? Imagine your Old World is Household Paint, and you set sail to explore the worlds of Marine Biology, Nanotechnology or Military Defense. Might you not bring back treasure in the form of exciting new technology?

Open Innovation

The notion that companies should seek technology outside their walls has been eloquently advanced by Henry Chesbrough in his book, *Open Innovation*.[1] He recounts Procter & Gamble's experience: They employed 8,600 scientists holding knowledge relevant to developing their new products. Yet there were 1.5 million scientists *outside* P&G with such knowledge. Their conclusion: "All the smart people don't work for us."[2]

To find these "smart people" and their ideas, you might want to use a solution broker... a service that connects solution seekers with solution providers. Here are three to check out:

> www.yet2.com Yet2.com is an online marketplace in which companies either out-license their technology or seek solutions to their technology problems. They also offer free technology alerts.

> www.ninesigma.com NineSigma helps solution-seeking companies draft requests-for-proposal, which it then distributes to an appropriate subset of its large global network of scientists.

> www.innocentive.com Innocentive works in a similar fashion to NineSigma, with the exception that the former delivers a *solution*, while the latter delivers several *solution proposals*.

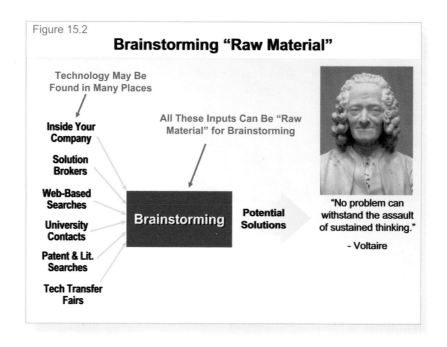

Figure 15.2

Brainstorming "Raw Material"

Technology May Be
Found in Many Places

All These Inputs Can Be "Raw
Material" for Brainstorming

Inside Your
Company

Solution
Brokers

Web-Based
Searches

University
Contacts

Patent & Lit.
Searches

Tech Transfer
Fairs

Brainstorming

Potential
Solutions

"No problem can
withstand the assault
of sustained thinking."

- Voltaire

A key element of good technical brainstorming is gathering the right raw material. You can do this in two ways. First, ask team members to screen technology in specific areas, as depicted in Figure 15.2. Second, engage individuals who already have knowledge in the areas relevant to your project. Do both of these and you're in for a great session, especially if you use this four-step process: 1) set up meeting, 2) generate and record ideas, 3) break old thinking patterns, and 4) prioritize ideas.

Step 1: Set Up Meeting

Begin by inviting four types of individuals. First, invite your project team members, who have already been thinking about the desired outcome and may have attractive solutions. Second, invite others from within your company who work in this technology space and are current in it. Third, invite "wild cards"—individuals who work elsewhere in your company, but are highly creative and able to bring fresh perspectives. Finally, consider inviting external experts—from universities, start-ups, recent retirement or elsewhere—to participate under a non-disclosure agreement.

In your invitations, lay out some history and a problem statement so participants can prepare. The latter should be concise and, in fact, may simply be the outcome statement you are focused on, e.g., "increase hiding power of a single coat of paint." Resist the urge to be "efficient" and tackle several outcomes at once; you will fail in "going deep" and succeed in confusing people. As you kick off your session, review the problem statement again, as well as the rules of brainstorming. Osborn's rules from more than a half-century ago still work nicely:

1) Do not criticize any idea.
2) Wild ideas are welcome.
3) The more ideas, the better.
4) Combine and build on others' ideas.

Step 2: Generate & Record Ideas

Begin your session by giving everyone 15 minutes to privately write as many ideas as they can. Then go around the room, letting each person read off one idea. Contributors can give brief explanations, and others can ask questions… but for *clarification* only, not judgment. As with Discovery Interviews, a Moderator facilitates this session while a Note-taker records each idea as it is read. The idea is projected for all to see using sticky notes similar to those used in Discovery Interviews (Figure 15.3).[3]

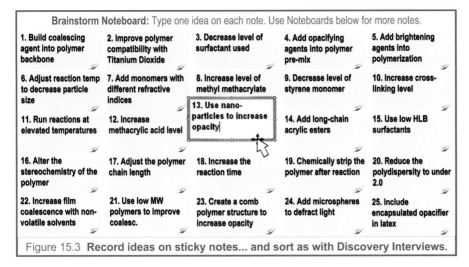

Figure 15.3 **Record ideas on sticky notes... and sort as with Discovery Interviews.**

The Moderator encourages participants to "springboard" off others' ideas, jotting down more ideas they can later read aloud. When the ideas dry up, it's time to move on to the third step.

Step 3: Break Old Thinking Patterns

Have you ever seen a new product and thought, "Brilliant! Now why didn't *I* think of that?" It could be your thinking was constrained by fixed mental models and unstated assumptions. Dr. Charles Prather (President of Bottom Line Innovation Associates, Inc.) does a fine job of facilitating and training teams to break free of these constraints.[4] He uses several trigger methods to "get out of the box" and generate fresh and unexpected ideas.

My favorite trigger method is "Reversing Hidden Assumptions." Figure 15.4 shows how this might work if you were spray-painting a plastic part and trying to minimize labor costs. First, hidden assumptions are listed, such as "We do the painting… we use spray application… the parts need to be painted" and so forth. Then these assumptions are reversed and the group asked to generate more ideas. Because the group has escaped the gravity of conventional thinking, it is common to generate more innovative ideas during this exercise than with the earlier brainstorming.

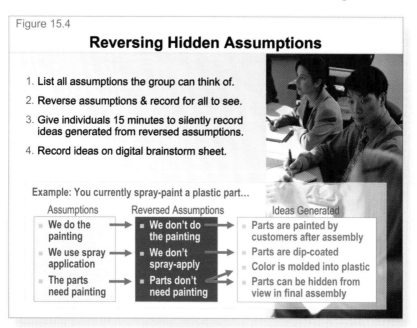

Figure 15.4

Reversing Hidden Assumptions

1. List all assumptions the group can think of.
2. Reverse assumptions & record for all to see.
3. Give individuals 15 minutes to silently record ideas generated from reversed assumptions.
4. Record ideas on digital brainstorm sheet.

Example: You currently spray-paint a plastic part...

Assumptions	Reversed Assumptions	Ideas Generated
We do the painting	We don't do the painting	Parts are painted by customers after assembly
We use spray application	We don't spray-apply	Parts are dip-coated
		Color is molded into plastic
The parts need painting	Parts don't need painting	Parts can be hidden from view in final assembly

Step 4: Prioritize Ideas

By this point, your group has likely generated hundreds of ideas and you need to prioritize them. New Product Blueprinting uses a two-step sorting process. First, Top Picks are dragged to the top of the Brainstorm Sheet… just as you did with Discovery Interviews. Try to reduce your list to a dozen or so of the best possible solutions.

Then the tool shown in Figure 15.5 is used. Your brainstormed Top Picks fill the green cells on the left, each numbered with a moveable red marker. On the right is a sorting matrix with the axes of "Likelihood of Solving Problem" and "Ease of Implementation." With the matrix projected on a screen, the brainstorming group directs the Moderator to drag each idea marker to the appropriate location. During this phase, we ask Mr. Osborn and his brainstorming rules to leave the room, so a healthy dose of wrangling and debate can occur.

The ideas that make their way to the northeast part of the matrix tend to be the most promising and are often included in the business case. To be clear, nobody *knows* that these ideas will work; that's why we have a development

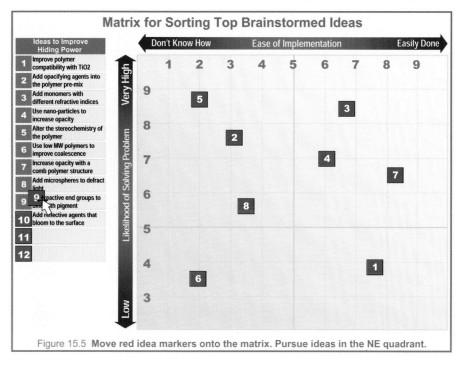

Figure 15.5 **Move red idea markers onto the matrix. Pursue ideas in the NE quadrant.**

stage that follows New Product Blueprinting. But when the team gets the green light to proceed into the costly development stage, they will have several promising technical paths to *immediately* begin pursuing.

A final note on technical brainstorming: If your business is global in nature, you probably find it difficult to get the right people in a conference room with a bunch of flip-chart pads and markers. The process we've just described is completely digital and is now routinely being done using web-conferences. This makes it much easier for you to engage the right people—inside and outside your company—when you need them most.

Endnotes

1.   Henry W. Chesbrough, *Open Innovation* (Boston: Harvard Business School Press, 2003).
2.   Ibid., p. xxvii.
3.   These are fictitious brainstorm ideas generated by the author for demonstration purposes only.
4.   Charles W. Prather, and Lisa K. Gundry, *Blueprints for Innovation* (New York: AMA Membership Publications, 1995).

Chapter 16

Step 7: Business Case

Who Needs the Business Case?
Twelve Sections to the Business Case
Beyond the Business Case

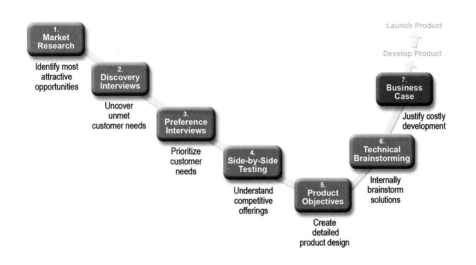

A business case completes the "front end" and helps your company decide if it should invest to *develop* the product. A business case is to a new product what a business plan is to a new company. In fact, venture capitalist (VC) thinking has been used to build the New Product Blueprinting business case template. Unlike most corporations, nearly all of the VC's money is at risk with new ventures, so VCs making poor investment decisions are quickly culled from the ranks. The surviving VCs provide an excellent model of investment decision-making.

Think of the business case as the most important gate in a Stage-Gate®[1] process. Some of our clients use a traditional four-to-seven stage process, while others use none. Regardless, we encourage them to have at least one gate separating two stages: the business case review between front-end work and product development (Figure 16.1). While the evidence for

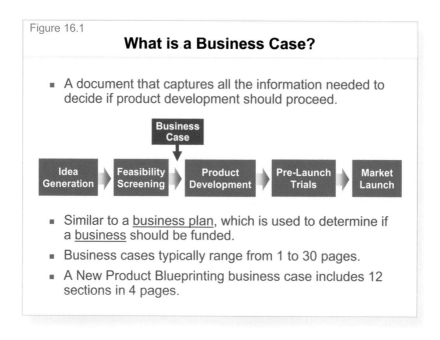

Figure 16.1

What is a Business Case?

- A document that captures all the information needed to decide if product development should proceed.

- Similar to a <u>business plan</u>, which is used to determine if a <u>business</u> should be funded.
- Business cases typically range from 1 to 30 pages.
- A New Product Blueprinting business case includes 12 sections in 4 pages.

stage-gate effectiveness is mixed, getting the up-front part right is known to be essential.[2] (If clients choose to keep their traditional stage-gate process, the Blueprinting business case is either attached to or replaces their old gate-review document.)

Who Needs the Business Case?

A good business case is needed by two groups: First, your team needs it. No one wants your project to succeed more than the team working on it. If it's going to crash and burn, the team should know this as soon as possible so they can start working on a winner instead. When team members construct their business case *as they go*, they'll see problems early... so they can either fix them or kill the project.

Second, your company's management badly needs standardized business cases so resources can be channeled to the most attractive opportunities. Picture this: In order to gain approval, a project team begins with a blank PowerPoint® presentation template.[3] Of twelve areas they should consider (which we'll discuss shortly), their project looks good on ten and miserable on two—let's say Competitive Landscape and Major Risks.

So what does the presentation look like? You guessed it: It's long on the ten strong areas and short—if not silent—on the two weak ones. So management, which has been burned or badly singed before, has to play a shell game: "What's missing... is it under *here*? Nope... how about under *here*?" Ridiculous? Sure. Commonplace? Absolutely.

It is a more sensible use of everyone's time, money and self-respect to be very clear about the standards for investing in new product development. When you implement this approach at your company, you will see an interesting metamorphosis. For a while, management may continue seeing some older presentations filled with undocumented assertions and wishful thinking. Then they'll see Blueprinting business cases that detail how many customers were interviewed, Market Satisfaction Gaps, results of competitive testing, etc. It won't be long before the former approach becomes a completely unacceptable means to allocate scarce resources.

Twelve Sections to the Business Case

After years of real-world refinement, we have reduced the business case to 12 sections (see Figure 16.2). The sequence of these sections is important.

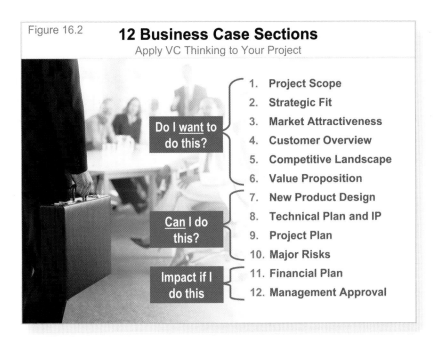

Figure 16.2

12 Business Case Sections
Apply VC Thinking to Your Project

Do I **want** to do this?
1. Project Scope
2. Strategic Fit
3. Market Attractiveness
4. Customer Overview
5. Competitive Landscape
6. Value Proposition

Can I do this?
7. New Product Design
8. Technical Plan and IP
9. Project Plan
10. Major Risks

Impact if I do this
11. Financial Plan
12. Management Approval

Imagine you are the decision-maker and are asked to invest in a project with a 60% internal rate of return. Would you do it? What if you are a jet engine-producer and the proposal is to develop a new frozen pizza? Obviously, you need to understand the project scope, strategic fit, etc. (Sections 1-6) to decide if you even *want* to do this. Once you are convinced, you'd like to know if you *can* do this (Sections 7-10). Only when this hurdle is crossed is the financial return (Section 11) relevant... so you can compare this project to other investment options.

Before taking a brief tour of these 12 sections, consider the business case writer and reader. Project teams are *always* pressed for time, and you don't want them staring at a blank screen trying to think of new charts to create. It helps to use an Excel-based template that provides the output with a minimal amount of input by the writer. After all, the team has already been loading most of the required data into an Excel file as they've progressed through the six preceding Blueprinting steps, so it need not be re-entered.

The reader—perhaps an executive—may be even more pressed for time, and often has a short attention span. We need a business case that is "short and filled with pictures." This is not meant to be insulting. Research by Dr. Richard Mayer (University of California) showed that placing text and related illustrations in close proximity dramatically improves comprehension and retention.[4] You don't have to present your business case this way... but if you don't, you'll be working *against* the way the reader's brain works best.

Each business case section (3 per page for a 4-page report) includes a quickly-absorbed illustration accompanied by a narrative explaining it. Just 5 of the 12 sections are reproduced in this book (see following blue-bordered Excel screen shots), but you'll get the idea.

1. Project Scope. Have you ever sat through a project review in which the presenter dove too deep too early and lost everyone? In this section, you introduce the team and give a brief *overview* of the project essentials: what will be developed, who will buy it, why they will buy it and how it will be used. If the team is excited about their project, they should let management know why they should feel the same.

2. Strategic Fit. Your project doesn't have to resemble everything else your company does today: If we always do what we always did, we'll always get what we always got, right? But companies get into hot water when they underestimate the new capabilities needed for new-to-the-company endeavors. In the illustration below, short blue bars beg for an explanation of how capabilities will be acquired. For this and all sections, the team would replace the text on the left with a narrative that describes their project.

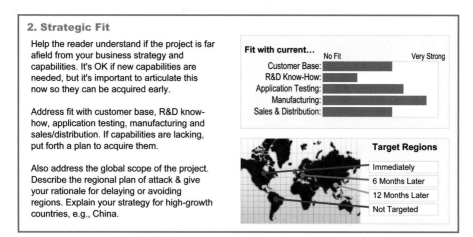

Also discuss the global scope of this project. What regions will you pursue, when will you pursue them, and what is your rationale for this strategy? Some regional businesses forget that the global economy can present significant new opportunities and threats... which should be considered here.

3. Market Attractiveness. It is critical that you clearly define and describe your market segment. Include the size of the market, market growth rate, and key market trends. Regional considerations, opportunities and threats should also be covered in this section.

These factors describe the attractiveness of the market... for any supplier. You should also make the reader aware of *your* company's involvement in this market. Is this a new market for you? If you already participate, what products do you sell and what is your current market share? How will you be able to leverage your current position?

4. Customer Overview. Key customers are reviewed in this market segment. As shown below, you'll describe your past dealings and future prospects with these customers. The pie chart size should match your market segment size with the five largest customers displayed; this communicates the level of customer concentration. You also identify any charter customers—those you plan to work especially closely with during product development. Additionally, you should communicate the number of customer interviews completed and describe their general reactions.

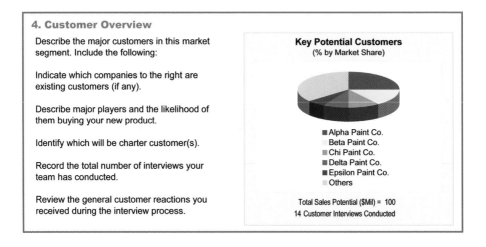

4. Customer Overview

Describe the major customers in this market segment. Include the following:

Indicate which companies to the right are existing customers (if any).

Describe major players and the likelihood of them buying your new product.

Identify which will be charter customer(s).

Record the total number of interviews your team has conducted.

Review the general customer reactions you received during the interview process.

Key Potential Customers
(% by Market Share)

- Alpha Paint Co.
- Beta Paint Co.
- Chi Paint Co.
- Delta Paint Co.
- Epsilon Paint Co.
- Others

Total Sales Potential ($Mil) = 100
14 Customer Interviews Conducted

5. Competitive Landscape. Here you describe the competition you'll face in this market segment, both from direct competitors and competing technologies or approaches customers consider viable. You should anticipate competitive reactions. We recommend assembling a "red team" of those most knowledgeable about the competition. They are charged with thinking like your toughest competitors and composing likely competitive reaction scenarios. How will you detect, prepare for and counterattack the most dangerous reaction scenarios?

6. Value Proposition. This is the most critical section… where you *quantitatively* communicate what customers are most eager to see improved. The value of this cannot be overstated. This is what prevents a company from spending millions on a new product customers won't buy. But it also provides a company with the confidence to aggressively invest in areas competitors just think about or dabble in.

Your Market Satisfaction Gap profile (from *Step 5: Product Objectives*) efficiently communicates what is important to customers—and what is not. For
the higher MSGs, briefly explain *why* customers want these outcomes.

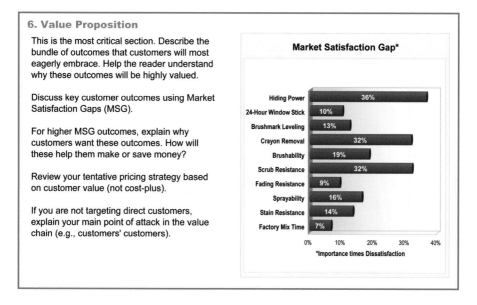

6. Value Proposition

This is the most critical section. Describe the bundle of outcomes that customers will most eagerly embrace. Help the reader understand why these outcomes will be highly valued.

Discuss key customer outcomes using Market Satisfaction Gaps (MSG).

For higher MSG outcomes, explain why customers want these outcomes. How will these help them make or save money?

Review your tentative pricing strategy based on customer value (not cost-plus).

If you are not targeting direct customers, explain your main point of attack in the value chain (e.g., customers' customers).

Market Satisfaction Gap*

Hiding Power	36%
24-Hour Window Stick	10%
Brushmark Leveling	13%
Crayon Removal	32%
Brushability	19%
Scrub Resistance	32%
Fading Resistance	9%
Sprayability	16%
Stain Resistance	14%
Factory Mix Time	7%

*Importance times Dissatisfaction

7. New Product Design. When was the last time you heard a team say *exactly*
what it wanted to develop? It is rare, and that's why many teams embark on
a "random walk" through the development stage that takes far longer than
expected. You will use the radar chart (from *Step 5: Product Objectives*) to
clearly communicate the intended new product design.

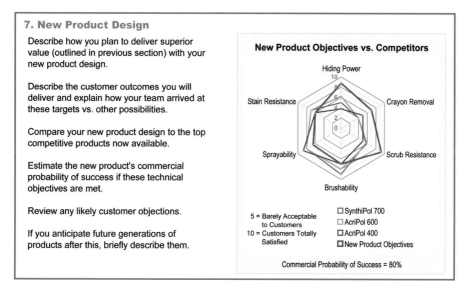

7. New Product Design

Describe how you plan to deliver superior value (outlined in previous section) with your new product design.

Describe the customer outcomes you will deliver and explain how your team arrived at these targets vs. other possibilities.

Compare your new product design to the top competitive products now available.

Estimate the new product's commercial probability of success if these technical objectives are met.

Review any likely customer objections.

If you anticipate future generations of products after this, briefly describe them.

New Product Objectives vs. Competitors

Hiding Power
Stain Resistance
Crayon Removal
Sprayability
Scrub Resistance
Brushability

5 = Barely Acceptable to Customers
10 = Customers Totally Satisfied

☐ SynthiPol 700
☐ AcriPol 600
☐ AcriPol 400
■ New Product Objectives

Commercial Probability of Success = 80%

This section also ties solutions directly to outcomes: Don't make fading resistance and factory mix time the cornerstones of your product design if the previous section said customers didn't care about these. The combination of Sections 6 and 7—what your customers want and what you intend to deliver—will bring a level of credibility and clarity to your business case that most reviewers have seldom seen.

8. Technical Plan and Intellectual Property. When you lay out your product design in Section 7, you create a huge question in the reader's mind: "So can we really *do* this?" Here you estimate that likelihood and explain several technical avenues to be pursued. These generally come directly from your work in *Step 6: Technical Brainstorming.*

You are not promising these ideas will work, but rather making a case to attempt them. In a sense, management will "buy an option" to try these technical paths, and can drop their option at a predetermined time if they become dead-end avenues. You also use this section to explain how you will protect your intellectual property.

9. Project Plan. The moment your project is approved, everyone on the team should know exactly what they will be doing the next day. Part of the beauty of a well-crafted business case is that it allows a team to attack the costly development stage instead of stumbling around in it. In this section, an overview is provided of "who does what and when." This is only a summary of major project elements; teams should also develop a more detailed project plan in which they aggressively manage the critical path to remove wasted weeks and months.[5]

10. Major Risks. Sure, nothing would ever go terribly wrong with your project... but if it *did*, what would it look like? Describe these "showstoppers" ... events that could significantly delay or kill your project. Also discuss the impact of the showstoppers on the project, early warning signs you will be watching for, and how their impact might be minimized or completely overcome. There is great value to both the reader and writer to think hard about this section.

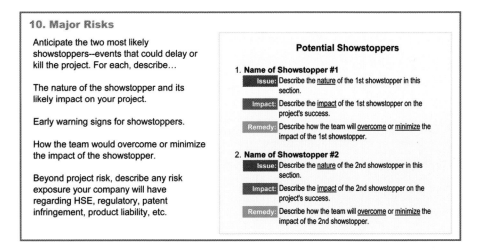

11. Financial Plan. This section includes a brief sales and income statement, capital request and measures of success—internal rate of return and net present value. The team doesn't need a financial wizard to create this. They just enter information they can answer better than anyone else: likely sales, price, project costs, etc. You're not shooting for precision at this point, but you do want to communicate your intentions and especially your underlying assumptions.

12. Management Approval. Too often project reviews end with this exchange: "So can we keep going?" "Sure. Good luck." That's just not good enough. Your team needs to ask for manpower, money, relief from other projects, or anything else you need to be wildly successful. Then agree upon the next checkpoint to update management on progress and review next steps. For instance, you might say you're going to pursue three technical paths described in Section 8 (Technical Plan) and will report on their viability in six months.

A closing thought on the business case: While it's designed for predevelopment reviews, you don't have to wait until that point in time before it sees the light of day. Many companies have regular project reviews (often monthly or quarterly), and their teams expend a lot of energy creating project review presentations. At these times, consider asking teams to simply project their business cases—in their current state of completion—directly from their Excel files. For each section, it's a good discipline to include in those left text boxes: 1) What we know (completed work), 2) what we think (to-be-validated), and 3) what we need to learn (to-be-determined), along with who will do what and when.

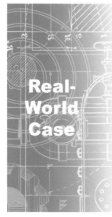

Real-World Case

After one of our earlier workshops, participants were having trouble "getting traction" for a variety of reasons. Then the business leader decided their monthly project reviews would no longer be "present-whatever-you-want," but would be based on each team's Blueprinting business case... *as it was being built.* This single change led to greater accountability, much shared learning, and far less preparation time (since they weren't creating new PowerPoint presentations each month).

Beyond the Business Case

The main deliverable of New Product Blueprinting is a business case to develop a blockbuster new product. But the incredible insight you have gained in your target market segment can yield important side-benefits as well. Beyond developing your next major new product, consider these actions:

1. Reposition existing products. Perhaps you have an existing product that satisfies key customer outcomes... but customers just don't realize it. How could you remedy this with rebranding, sales force training, or new promotional literature?

2. Modify existing products. Do you have a product that is over-designed... ripe for cost reduction by eliminating outcomes customers don't care about? Or maybe it lacks just one key outcome that could be quickly met with small adjustments.

3. Refocus target market. Does your targeted "cluster of customers" need updating? Sometimes companies have been averaging the needs of too large a group and not fully satisfying any. In other cases, they have simply overlooked an attractive segment with significant unmet needs.

4. Revise business model. Sometimes interviews will uncover customer outcomes that could be satisfied with means other than a new product: introducing new industry standards or helping customers enter new geographies, for example. These may lead you to a different organization structure, new channel partners, a business acquisition, etc.

5. Reprioritize project pipeline. In light of what you have learned in this market segment, changes may be called for in your new product pipeline. Which projects should be accelerated... modified in scope... dropped? Your new "outside-in" learning gives you a wonderful opportunity to free up needed resources for the most important projects.

6. Build patent hedge. Occasionally, you uncover an outcome so critical to the future of a market segment that you'd like to corner the market on it... legally of course. You may be able to do this by studying the existing patent landscape, creating a thoughtful patent strategy and investing in key technology.

At a project level, you are done. Your business case is complete and you've considered the six side-benefits above. You'll hang up your Blueprinting tools until the next project, and proceed into the product development and launch stages.

At another level, you may just be getting started. Changing your company's DNA to drive sustainable organic growth happens neither quickly nor easily. But there is nothing else you can do that will make your company as attractive to invest in, as rewarding to purchase from, as difficult to compete against, and as much fun to work at. It is my sincere wish that what you have learned in these pages will contribute to your success.

Endnotes

1. The term Stage-Gate® was coined by Dr. Robert Cooper and is a registered trademark of the Product Development Institute, Inc.

2. Paige Leavitt, ed., *Improving New Product Development Performance and Practices* (Houston: APQC International Benchmarking Clearinghouse, 2003). This APQC benchmarking study did not find a significant correlation between the use of a stage-gate type of process and new product success, yet did find such a relationship in 77 other practices. Many of the practices found to correlate most strongly with success are performed largely or completely in the front-end of product development.

3. PowerPoint® is a registered trademark of The Microsoft Corporation.

4. A series of tests compared subjects' understanding and retention of information in two cases: 1) text only and 2) text with illustrations. The use of text with illustrations improved understanding by an average of 89%, and retention by 23% on average. In another series of tests, subjects were exposed to text and illustrations that were either near each other or spaced apart from each other. Placing text and illustrations near each other improved understanding by an average of 68% and retention by 42% on average. See Richard E. Mayer, *Multi-Media Learning*, (New York: Cambridge University Press, 2001), 72-76, 88-92.

5. For complex projects, we recommend using Microsoft Project® to create a project Gantt chart. After an initial draft is created, the entire team should use a digital projector to review the time-lines, dependencies and responsibilities for all tasks. Special attention should be given to accelerating those tasks on the critical path—the rate-limiting sequence of tasks for the entire project. For less complex projects, a simple Excel-based Gantt chart is helpful.

How AIM Can Help

If you feel reasonably good about your existing new product development process, I hope you have picked up some useful tips to enhance it. Our staff at Advanced Industrial Marketing, Inc., (AIM) will be happy to answer any questions you may have on the finer points.

If you would like more help from AIM, here's how we usually do that best: We don't do your work—such as customer interviewing—for you... because you wouldn't learn new skills. And we avoid stand-alone workshops where the instructor parachutes in, teaches and moves on... because little learning would "stick." We *are* very excited about helping clients build and use new skills over several months. This approach requires a modest level of overall training time; then we get out of your way.

New Product Blueprinting Workshop. We conduct a 2-3-day private workshop at your office or nearby facility for 8-25 participants—who are arranged in small project teams. Participants alternate between lecture and break-out rooms, where they advance real projects through the Blueprinting steps. Afterwards, teams a) conduct real customer interviews, b) return for the final 1-2-day workshop several months later, and c) continue driving toward their business case. Throughout the process, a dedicated AIM coach conducts monthly follow-up web-conferences and supports teams as requested. (If you want to develop internal coaches—a practice we strongly encourage—we accommodate that as well.)

Blueprinter™ **Software**. The blue-bordered screen shots you've seen in this book were all created in Microsoft Excel. To save time for B2B suppliers, we have integrated these and all Blueprinting steps into a single Excel file called Blueprinter... which all workshop participants receive. It is designed to boost your implementation of New Product Blueprinting in five ways:

1) *Time Savings.* Since your people are most likely running ragged, you want them to be as efficient as possible; Blueprinter saves days of data-crunching, chart-making and report-writing.

2) *Embedded Learning.* After teams receive training, Blueprinter reinforces key learnings with reminders and a step-by-step, easy-to-follow plan of action.

3) *Common Language.* Your organization moves to another level of effectiveness as team members share a common language and process that are reinforced with Blueprinter.

4) *Corporate Memory.* One client calls Blueprinter software the "lab notebook for marketers." Instead of data being scattered about, it's all contained in one Blueprinter file per project... from initial market research to final business case.

5) *Impressed Customers.* The screen views projected during interviews display your company name, and there's often a "wow" factor when your well-trained teams interview using Blueprinter.

This is an exciting time for B2B suppliers to drive organic growth... by adopting new methods their competitors still lack. I wish you great success in your journey! If you have questions or we can help in any way, please visit www.newproductblueprinting.com for up-to-date contact information.

Bibliography

Brue, Gregg, and Robert G. Launsby. *Design for Six Sigma.* New York: McGraw-Hill, 2003.

Burchill, Gary, and Christina Hepner Brodie. *Voices into Choices: Acting on the Voice of the Customer.* Madison, WI: Joiner Associates, 1997.

Camp, Justin J. *Venture Capital Due Diligence: A Guide to Making Smart Investment Choices and Increasing Your Portfolio Returns.* New York: John Wiley and Sons, 2002.

Chesbrough. Henry. *Open Innovation: The New Imperative for Creating and Profiting from Technology.* Boston, MA: Harvard Business School Press, 2003.

Christensen, Clayton M., and Michael E. Raynor. *The Innovator's Solution: Creating and Sustaining Successful Growth.* Boston, MA: Harvard Business School Press, 2003.

Christensen, Clayton M. *The Innovator's Dilemma: When New Technologies Cause Great Firms to Fail.* Boston, MA: Harvard Business School Press, 1997.

Cooper, Robert G. *Winning at New Products: Accelerating the Process from Idea to Launch.* 2nd Ed. Reading, MA: Addison-Wesley Publishing Company, 1993.

Cooper, Robert G. *Winning at New Products: Accelerating the Process from Idea to Launch.* 3rd Ed. New York: Perseus Books, 2001.

Eales-White, Rupert. *Ask the Right Question: How to Get What You Want Every Time and in Any Situation.* New York: McGraw-Hill, 1998.

Hlavacek, James D. *Profitable Top-Line Growth for Industrial Companies: How to Make Any Industrial Firm Grow Profitably.* The American Book Company, 2002.

Hofstede, Geert. *Cultural Consequences: Comparing Values, Behaviors, Institutions, and Organizations Across Nations.* 2nd Ed. Thousand Oaks, CA: Sage Publications, 2001.

Kirton, M. J. *Adaption-Innovation: In the Context of Diversity and Change.* London: Routledge, 2003.

Lajoux, Alexandra Reed. *The Art of M&A Integration: A Guide to Merging Resources, Processes & Responsibilities.* 2nd Ed. New York: McGraw-Hill, 2006.

Leavitt, Paige, ed. *Improving New Product Development Performance and Practices.* Houston, TX: American Productivity and Quality Center, 2003.

Mayer, Richard E. *Multimedia Learning.* New York: Cambridge University Press, 2001.

McQuarrie, Edward F. *Customer Visits: Building a Better Market Focus.* 2nd Ed. Thousand Oaks, CA: Sage Publications, 1998.

Prather, Charles W., and Lisa K. Gundry. *Blueprints for Innovation: How Creative Processes Can Make You and Your Company More Competitive.* New York: AMA Membership Publications, 1995.

Rackham, Neil. *Spin Selling.* New York: McGraw-Hill, 1988.

ReVelle, Jack B., John W. Moran, and Charles A. Cox. *The QFD Handbook.* New York: John Wiley & Sons, 1998.

Shenkar, Oded. *The Chinese Century: The Rising Chinese Economy and Its Impact on the Global Economy, the Balance of Power, and Your Job.* Upper Saddle River, NJ: Wharton School Publishing, 2005.

Shillito, M. Larry. *Acquiring, Processing, and Deploying Voice of the Customer.* Boca Raton: St. Lucie Press, 2001.

Terminko, John. *Step-by-Step QFD: Customer-Driven Product Design.* 2nd. Ed. Boca Raton, FL: St. Lucie Press, 1997.

Ulwick, Anthony W. *What Customers Want: Using Outcome-Driven Innovation to Create Breakthrough Products and Services.* New York: McGraw-Hill, 2005.

Weinstein, Art. *Handbook of Market Segmentation: Strategic Targeting for Business and Technology Firms.* 3rd. Ed. New York: The Hawthorn Press, 2004.

Index

#

1800s, 149

1885, 105, 150

1940s, 178

1970s, 49, 68

1971, 49

1980s, 19, 71

2003, 7

20th Century, 7, 71

3M, 133

A

A.T. Kearney, 27

Absentee landlords, 22

Acquisitions, 1, 22-23, 27, 78

Activity, 139-141

Advanced Industrial Marketing, 106, 129, 197-198

Agenda, 133, 145

AIM. *See* Advanced Industrial Marketing.

Airline, 19

Algorithms, 127

Amazon.com, 124

American Productivity & Quality Center, 7, 68, 95, 196

Amusement park rides, 74

Architects, 37-39, 43

Argon gas, 16

Arrogance, 132

Assumptions, 5, 41, 47, 57, 64-65, 142, 182

B

B2B. *See* Business to business.

B2C. *See* Business to consumer.

Background, 143-144

Banners, 100

Barely acceptable outcome, 153, 164

Battleground markets. *See* Market, battleground.

Benefits Map, 147, 150

Bias, 5, 41, 47, 132, 161-162, 172

Bicycles, 59

Blockbuster product. *See* Product, blockbuster.

Blueprinting steps, 40-41

Body language, 43, 136, 141

Boston Consulting Group, 27, 79

Bottom Line Innovation Associates Inc., 182

Brainstorming. *See* Technical, brainstorming.

Branding, 93, 194

Breadth of applications, 14

Breakthrough Polymers, 126

Budget, 55

Builders, 21-27

Burning-platform rationale, 99

Business books, 98

Business case, 4-5, 40-41, 45, 47, 110, 185-196

    sections of, 187-194

    template, 66

    who needs, 186-187

Business model, 195

Business to business, 2, 5, 75, 105, 116

    vs. business to consumer, 2-3, 11-20, 117-118

Business to consumer, 2-3, 11-20, 85, 117-118

Business types, 116-118

Buyer

    dynamics, 13

    engagement. *See* Customer, engagement.

    number, 13

Buying behaviors spectrum, 12

C

Cabinet coatings, 76, 126

Capacity, 137

Cars, 22

CAT scan machine, 44

Cathedrals, 23

Change, 3-4, 33, 98-99

Chemical companies, 118

Chesbrough, Henry, 58, 179

Chess, 61

China, 56, 59

Christensen, Clayton, 31, 95

Clarification, 145

Clusters of customers. *See* Customers, clusters of.

Coaching, 47, 101

Coatings, 76, 126, 128

Collaboration, 14, 47, 75, 84, 117

Colorants, 14

Comfort, 145

Commitment, 139

Commoditization, 3-4, 24, 54

    two principles of, 25

Company growth, 3, 45, 121

    organic, 2, 21-22, 195

Competition, 1, 5, 7, 11, 18, 24, 29, 33-34, 43, 54-55, 77, 84, 93-94, 103, 107, 147, 162

    capabilities, 159

    global, 55-56

    inter-customer, 117

    landscape, 190

    off-shore, 4, 16, 55

    position of, 69

Completion, 145

Concentration, 73, 78-79

Conjoint analysis, 116

Consolidation, 22

Construction equipment, 128

Consultant studies, 125

Consumer goods, 12, 19, 39, 152, 157

Context, 145

Converge, 152

Cooper and Kleinschmidt, 59

Cooper, Robert G., 49, 71, 196

Coronary bypass surgery. See Heart surgery.

Corporate memory, 47

Cost, 70

    effective, 120

    labor, 137, 182

    reduction, 55, 137, 171

    structure, 55

Creative foresight, 37-38

Credibility, 19

Cultural sensitivity, 136

Current state, 146

Customer, 1, 5

    charter, 190

    collaborate with, 14-15

    concentration, 190

    clusters of, 76, 115, 195

    definition, 19

    engagement, 13, 15, 90, 132, 142, 144-145, 150

    face time, 43, 83, 157

    interaction, 109

    interviews. See Interviews.

    intimacy, 55-56

    needs. *See* Needs.

    outcomes, 44-46, 48-49, 67, 136-137, 143-144, 151-153, 161-162, 164, 169

    overview, 190

    panel, 116

    relationships with, 14

    satisfaction, 44

    specifications, 165

    tours, 19, 137-138

    value, 6, 107

D

Data gathering, 156-157

Death spiral, 54-55

Deming, Edward, 64, 71, 100

Demolition, 128

Detailed plan, 37

Differentiation, 1-3, 7, 16, 24-25, 97, 107, 178

Digital projection, 17, 46, 89-91, 100, 126, 135, 142, 145, 148, 157, 167

Discovery interviews. See Interviews.

Disruptive innovation, 35

Distribution, 30

Diverge, 152

Diversity of knowledge, 102

Due diligence, 129

Dun and Bradstreet, 123

E

Earth-moving equipment, 74, 128

Ebbinghaus, Hermann, 105, 150

Education, 39, 102

E-mail, 90, 133, 150

Emotional buying, 13

Employee
    cost, 137
    development, 97-106
    training, 101

Encyclopedia of Associations, 125

Engagement. See Customer, engagement.

Engineering, 12, 15, 26, 124, 175

Europe, Western, 136

EWorkMarkets.com, 124

Exclusivity, 93

Experience, 39

Expression, 139-141

Eye contact, 141

F

Fabric, 163

Facts, 64-67, 158
    misinterpreted, 64, 67
    missing, 66-67
    poorly analyzed, 64-65
    undiscovered, 64, 67
    wrong, 64-65

Fads, 21, 23

Failure modes, 29-32, 143

Feed hopper, 26

Final consumer, 14

Financial reports, 22, 26,104, 187, 193

Focus group, 11, 14, 19, 116-117

Follow-through, 103

Follow-up, 101, 149

Food coloring, 14

Footrace, 82, 84

Forestry, 128

Forklift trucks, 74

Fortune 500, 124

Freedonia Group, 123

Front end of development, 1-2, 6, 14, 42, 46-47, 68, 97, 118, 185, 196
    upgrading, 69-72
    valuation errors, 64-67

Frost and Sullivan, 123

Furniture coatings, 76

G

Gale Group, 125

Gantt chart, 196

Garbage, 74

GE/McKinse Matrix, 79

Germany, 90, 150

Global, 121
    economy, 55-56, 78, 189
    strategy, 107

Gold, 45

Golf, 23

Goodall, Jane, 17

Google, 122

Government regulation, 66, 121, 143

Great Hope projects, 56-57

Greeks, 140

Green Book, The, 125

Grisham, John, 5

Growth. *See* Company growth.

Guideline, 124

Gym floor coatings, 76, 128

H

Hart, Basil Liddell, 73

Heart surgery, 98, 101

Healthcare, 124

Hewlett-Packard, 15, 19

Hiring

    delays, 26

Hlavacek, Jim, 150

Hofstede, Geert, 136

Homebuilding, 37-38, 117

Hoses, 12, 18

House of Quality, 47

Huthwaite Corporation, 15

Hydraulic cylinder markets, 74

I

Idea generation, 5, 17, 46-47, 89-90, 134, 136, 142, 180-183

Ideal state, 146

Illustration, 188, 196

Implementation, 6, 103

Importance rating, 18, 132, 154, 168-170

Incrementalism, 53-59

Industrial goods, 12

Industry experts, 124

Industry reputation, 93

Information brokers, 122

IngentaConnect.com, 123

Innocentive, 179

Innovation, 35, 49, 56, 98

    open, 58, 179-180

Inota, 124

Insurance, 118

Intellectual property, 43, 45-46, 192

Interest, 139

Interior decorators, 22

Internet, 41, 47, 100, 108, 116, 118

    surveys, 82

Interview, 17-18, 21, 25, 33-34, 43-45, 49, 58-59, 70, 81-95, 99-101, 109, 116, 118, 119, 121-122, 127, 190

    customer-directed, 46

    data review, 168-171

    debriefing, 47, 90, 148-150

    discovery, 4-5, 16, 20, 40-41, 131-150

    equipment, 135

    logistics, 132-137

    market-proactive, 83-84

    objectives, 133

    preference, 4-5, 40-41, 150,

    questions, 86, 140, 143, 153

    roles, 133

    script, 133

    setting up, 133-134

    shortcomings, 86-87

    structure, 145-148

    who should conduct, 133

J

Japan, 56

Judgment

    suspending, 139

K

KAI. *See* Kirton Adaption-Innovation.

Kanan, Dean, 179

Kirton Adaption-Innovation, 100-103, 105

Kirton, Michael, 111

Knowledge, 179

KPMG, 27

L

Labor cost, 137, 182

Laptop, 17, 100, 135, 149, 157

Large-ticket items, 15

Library, 120, 125

Life cycle. *See* Product, life cycle.

Listening, 45, 86, 100

    skills, 138-141

Low-end disruption, 31, 35, 158

M

Machine end, 26-27

Mail survey. *See* Survey, mail.

Management approval, 193

Manufacturing, 2, 6, 71, 98, 135

Marine biology, 179

Market research flow chart, 119-120

Market, 4

    analysis, 7, 68, 76

    attractive segments of, 5, 79, 82, 97, 108, 119, 125, 187, 189

    battleground, 73-79

    growth, 121

    penetration, 110

    reaction, 47

    research, 4-5, 7, 40-41, 45, 65, 70, 73, 108, 115-129, 145

    satisfaction gap, 153-156, 170-171, 187, 191

    segmentation, 16, 18-19, 25, 30, 34, 40-41, 45-46, 73-79, 99, 108, 118, 120-121, 124, 157-158

    share, 70, 97, 107

    size, 120

    target, 26, 30, 109, 115, 126-127, 162, 195

    trends, 120

Marketing, 75, 135

MarketResearch.com, 122

Mayer, Richard, 188

McKinsey, 27

McQuarrie, Edward F., 19

Memory, 105, 150

Metal stamping equipment, 74

Metrics

    process, 104

    result, 104

Microsoft Excel, 7, 47, 126, 146, 165, 167-168, 188, 194, 196

Microsoft PowerPoint, 186

Microsoft Project, 196

Microwave oven, 44, 59

Military defense, 179

Mind-set, 99-101

Moderator, 133, 135, 140, 146, 181-183

Motivation, 99

Must-have, 146, 165

Nail polish, 14

Nanotechnology, 179

N

Needs, 1, 15, 18, 24-26, 29-30, 33, 39, 47, 49, 59, 67, 78, 82, 84, 103, 108, 118, 120-121, 162

    prioritizing, 119

    uncovering, 132

New product development diagnostic. *See* Product, development diagnostic.

New World, 179

New-market disruptions, 35

New-product machine. *See* Product, machine.

NineSigma, 179

Non-disclosure agreement, 136, 180

North America, 136

Note-taker, 133, 135, 146, 149, 181

O

Observer, 133, 135

Obvious Zone, 92-94

Old World, 179

Omissions, 5, 41

OneSource, 123

One-way mirrors, 17

Open innovation. See Innovation.

Operational efficiency, 1

Organic growth. *See* Business growth.

Osborn, Alex, 178, 183

Outcomes. *See* Customer, outcomes.

Outside-insight, 4, 47, 154, 167, 171-172, 174-175

P

Packaging, 137

Paint, 63, 122, 126-127, 131, 134-135, 144, 167-168, 172, 182

Paper, 13

Pareto chart, 67

Passion, 24

Patents, 32-33, 92-93, 195

Paving, 128

PEAR method, 139-141

People, 16, 179

Personal interests, 22-23

Petrochemicals, 26

Pharmaceuticals, 14, 32

Plastics, 11, 14

Ponzi scheme, 23

Post-It Notes, 133

Posture, 139-141

Prather, Charles, 182

Preference interview. *See* Interviews.

Pre-sell, 15-16, 20

Pricing, 5, 30-33, 35, 41, 54-55, 69-70, 82, 92-93, 147, 156, 161

    negotiations, 24

    optimal, 18

    tentative strategy, 191

    unit, 24-25

Print paste, 13, 16

Printing, 56

Prison, 24

Procter & Gamble, 58, 179

Product

    attributes, 18, 88

    benefits, 15

    blockbuster, 29-30, 41, 54, 194

    breakthrough vs. incremental, 58-59

    definition, 19

    design, 5, 13, 15, 18, 40, 44, 47, 62, 155, 173-174, 191-192

    development diagnostic, 106-111

    differentiation, 1-3, 7, 16, 24-25

    dominant, 92-94

    failure. See Failure modes.

    features, 15

    launch, 11, 13, 63, 68

    leading, 92-94

    life cycle, 24-25

    long-shot, 92-94

    machine, 61-72, 98-99, 158

    me-too, 24-25, 92-94, 107

    objectives, 4, 40-41, 45, 47, 110, 167-175, 174

    off-the-shelf, 159

    pipeline, 32, 195

    pre-sell of. *See* Pre-sell.

    pricing. *See* Pricing.

    prototype, 15

    repositioning existing, 194

    specialty, 3, 25

    success, 33-35, 71, 92, 97

    tweaks, 53-54, 99, 194

    types, 92-84

    value. See Value.

    vs. service, 19

Product Development and Management Association, 125

Productivity, 7

Profit, 55, 93, 120, 147

    maximizing, 29-35

Profound.com, 123

Progress

    measurement of, 104-105

Project

    plan, 192

    scope, 127-128, 188

Projections, 67

Promotion, 13, 69, 75

Purchasing agents, 24-25, 54

Q

Quality, 1, 7, 137

Quality Function Deployment, 46, 116

R

Rackham, Neil, 19-20
Rational buying, 13-14
Raw material, 137, 180
Realtors, 22
Reconnaissance, 73
Recycling, 137
Refrigerators, 59
Regulation. *See* Government regulation.
Regulatory roadblock, 66
Research
    and Development Department, 1, 3, 34, 55-56, 62-63, 81, 94, 135, 174-175
    objectives, 118-119
    published, 122
    secondary tools, 122-125
    see also Market, research.
Resources, 18, 26, 30, 35, 55, 61, 63
    allocating scarce, 187
    strategically aiming, 16
    wasted, 35, 46, 91
Response, 139-141
Restaurants, 117
Retention, 188, 196
Reverse auction, 24
Risk
    major, 192-193
    paradox, 53-54
    reduce, 57-58
Role-playing, 101
Roofing shingles, 11
Rubber, 26
Running blindfolded, 142

S

Sales force, 1, 135, 194
Satisfaction rating, 18, 132, 154, 168-170
Scared Straight, 24
Science, 124
Search engines, 122

Segway, 179
Selling, 19-20, 24-25, 42-43, 46, 136
Seminar, 101
Service, 1, 19
Shaw, George Bernard, 100
Sheds, 23
Shoes, 59
Showstoppers, 66, 192-193
Side-by-side testing. See Testing.
Six Sigma, 7, 46, 62, 84, 116
Skilled generalists, 125
Slogans, 100
Socio-economic differences, 16
Soda, 11-12
Solutions, 44-46, 48-49, 136-137, 143-144, 177-184
    vs. outcomes, 44-45
Specialty, 3
    semi-, 25
    vs. commodity, 25
Spectrum of buying behaviors, 12
Stage-gate process, 46, 68, 71, 185-186, 195
Statistical Process Control, 7, 71
Statistics, 18
Stockholders, 2, 27
Storage units, 13
Strategic fit, 189
Strategic market segment portfolio, 77-78
Success modes, 33-34
Sun Tzu, 70
Super Bowl, 11
Supplier dependency, 13-14
Survey, 156-157
    internet, 82
    mail, 82, 116
    methods, 82
    telephone, 82, 116

T

Tape recording, 17, 47

Taxi driver, 56

Team

    accountability, 110

    diversity, 108

    meetings, 180-181

    multi-functional vs. mono-functional, 102

    red, 190

Technical brainstorming, 4-5, 40-41, 45, 47, 91, 103, 110, 146, 177-184

Technical plan, 192

Technically savvy, 12, 14

Technology, 26, 31, 38, 54, 58, 65, 110, 121, 127, 137, 156, 160, 162, 175

    development vs. product development, 178-179

Telephone survey. *See* Survey, telephone.

Television sets, 59

Tell-and-sell communication, 83

Testing, 18, 47, 153, 156

    data, 163-166, 171-173

    competitive, 109

    converting results to ratings, 164

    customer-centric, 161-163

    side-by-side, 4-5, 40, 45, 48, 154, 159-166, 171-173

Theory of Non-Obviousness, 92-94

Thinking, 100, 148, 180

Time, 22, 24-25, 27, 42

    development, 69

    to market, 70

Tools, 6-7

Toothpaste, 13, 16

Top picks, 148-149

Totally satisfied, 153, 164

Tours, 109, 137-138

Toys, 59

Trade secrets, 107

Trade shows, 135

Training, 26, 48, 101, 194

Travel, 70

Trends, 120-121, 143

Trigger methods, 145-146

Turtle, 140

Turtling, 140, 142, 146

Tyranny of the Urgent, 98

U

U.S. Military, 88

Ulwick, Anthony W., 44, 49, 150

United Kingdom, 16

University of California, 188

Unmet needs. *See* Needs.

Up-front work, 107

V

Valuation errors, 64-67

Value, 5, 21-23, 29-31, 53, 74, 82, 143

    chain, 14, 19, 87, 108, 128, 134-135, 161

    negative net present, 31

    proposition, 66, 69, 107, 120-121, 127, 187, 190-191

Value-in-use, 24-25, 161, 171

Venture capital, 66, 71, 110, 185

VOC. *See* Voice-of-the-customer.

Voice-of-ourselves, 84

Voice-of-the-customer, 2, 5, 17-18, 46-49, 84, 98, 142-143, 145

W

Washers, 59

Waste, 137

What Customers Want, 44

What-if product designs, 47, 174

Wheat, 128

Wild cards, 180

Wishful thinking, 5, 41

Work-arounds, 138

Workshops, 47, 101

Y

Yet2.com, 179

Z

Zinc coatings, 16